Sermons on Prayer

Sermons on Prayer

Outlines and Messages

Ronald E. Wall

BAKER BOOK HOUSE 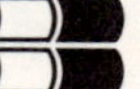
Grand Rapids, Michigan 49506

ISBN: 0-8010-9672-3

Printed in the United States of America

Contents

PART TWO **"Pray as I Pray"**

Preface

Sermons on Prayer: Outlines and Messages is not written in technical language for scholars and theologians but in simple and understandable language for laymen and preachers who want to study again the teachings of Jesus on prayer and who want to learn how to pray more effectively.

Nearly all this material was used in sermons in the College Park Baptist Church of Greensboro, North Carolina, where I had the privilege of preaching and serving as pastor for over fifteen years. Several of these messages were delivered over live television at the Sunday morning worship service. It is my earnest prayer that they may be a blessing as they are read by others.

Here the biblical quotations are from the Revised Standard Version, which is more accurate than the beautiful King James Version. All these messages are based directly on the Scriptures, because I believe with the apostle Paul that "the sacred writings . . . are able to instruct you for salvation through faith in Christ Jesus" (2 Tim. 3:15).

I am grateful to those who have granted permission to use copyright material and for friends who have graciously read the manuscript and made helpful suggestions. These include Mrs. Claud B. Bowen, Dr. Carlton S. Prickett, retired pastor; my wife Esther and my daughter Paddy Sue Wells.

Outlines for Sermons

1
The God to Whom We Pray

"Pray then like this: Our Father who art in heaven, Hallowed be thy name" (Matt. 6:9).

I. He lives in heaven.

1. Heaven is where God dwells.
2. Heaven is a symbol of beauty, truth, goodness, love, kindness, mercy, righteousness, and glory.
3. We need not shout in order to be heard.

II. God is perfect.

1. He is morally perfect.
2. He is perfect in knowledge, wisdom, and understanding.
3. He is perfect in love and power.

III. God is holy.
"Hallowed be thy name." He is to be reverenced, loved, and worshiped.

IV. He is a God who knows our needs and provides for them.

V. He is the God who rewards us.
VI. He is the forgiving Heavenly Father.
VII. He is the God who is to be glorified by our living.
VIII. He is the Sovereign Lord whose will we are to do.

2
The Kingdom of God

"Thy kingdom come" (Matt. 6:10).

I. What is the kingdom of God?
   1. It is primarily spiritual, not material.
   2. Paul describes it in spiritual terms.
   3. It is universal in scope and purpose.
   4. It is heavenly in origin,
   5. but it comes down to earth.
   6. It will have outward manifestations.

II. The coming of the Kingdom.
   1. The time of its coming.
   2. How does the kingdom come?
   3. What are we to do about bringing it in?
   4. It is a growing kingdom.

III. God is the King of the Kingdom.
   1. Many Old Testament prophets speak of the coming King, who is the Messiah.
   2. Jesus Christ came as the King of love and truth.

IV. Who are the subjects of the Kingdom?
   1. Some cannot enter it.
      (1) Those who have not been born again.
      (2) The hypocrites.
      (3) The proud and arrogant.
      (4) The unrighteous.
      (5) Those who trust in riches.
   2. Who then can enter?

(1) Those who have had a spiritual birth.
(2) Those who do God's will.
(3) The poor in spirit, the humble.
(4) The persecuted.
(5) Those who come to Christ in childlike faith.

3
The Will of God

"Thy will be done, On earth as it is in heaven" (Matt. 6:10).

I. Jesus, God's Son, lived by God's will completely.

1. He sought to know and to do God's will (John 5:30).
2. He came to earth to do God's will.
3. Fear of death did not turn him aside.
4. By doing God's will he won a great victory.

II. What is God's will for us?

1. His will is his desire and purpose for us.
2. His will is always in keeping with his character.
3. We can discover God's will by prayer and Bible study.
4. Some difficult questions arise about God's will.
5. We can know without a doubt what God's will is for us.

III. What are the results of doing God's will?

1. We enter the kingdom of God.
2. We become akin to Jesus Christ, and members of God's family.
3. It gives a unifying purpose to life.
4. We may have to suffer, but such suffering will not be in vain.
5. Our lives will be a blessing to others.

4
Our Daily Bread

"Give us this day our daily bread" (Matt. 6:11).

I. While bread is important, some things come before bread.

1. God comes first. "Our Father who art in heaven."
2. His name comes first, "Hallowed be thy name."
3. His kingdom comes before bread. "Thy kingdom come."
4. God's will comes before bread. "Thy will be done."

II. We are dependent upon God to supply bread.

1. This petition is addressed to God, creator and owner of all things.
2. How shall we get food for our bodies?
   (1) We are to ask God for it.
   (2) We are to work for it.

III. This petition forbids selfish praying for bread.

1. We are to recognize the needs and rights of all people for bread.
2. Jesus forbids us to live selfishly.

IV. This petition reminds us that Jesus is the "Bread of life."

1. It does not refer primarily to bread for the body.
2. Jesus said: "Work not (exclusively) for the food which perishes, but for the bread that endures until eternal life, which the Son of man shall give unto you.
3. As bread is necessary for the body, so spiritual food is necessary for the soul"

5
Forgiveness of Sins

"And forgive us our debts, As we also have forgiven our debtors. . . . For if you forgive men their trespasses, your heavenly Father also will forgive you; but if you do not forgive men their trespasses, neither will your Father forgive your trespasses" (Matt. 6:12, 14, 15).

I. We need to pray for divine forgiveness.
   1. We have all sinned.
   2. Because unforgiveness is a fatal disease.

II. What are the conditions of divine forgiveness?
   1. We must confess our sins to God and repent.
   2. We must believe on Jesus Christ who made atonement for our sins on his cross.
   3. We must be forgiving in *our* attitudes and actions if we are to receive forgiveness.

III. To pray this prayer sincerely is to receive forgiveness.

6
God's Guidance and Deliverance

"And lead us not into temptation, But deliver us from evil" (Matt. 6:13).

I. The origin and nature of temptation.
   1. God does not tempt us to do evil.
   2. God permits us to be tested.
   3. The devil is the origin of evil, including temptation.
   4. A person is tempted to do the evil that dwells in his heart.
   5. We may be tempted by our foes and also by our friends.
   6. We may be tempted, not only at our weakest points, but also at our strongest.
   7. We are tempted from without and from within.
   8. We all are tempted at times.

II. Our defense against temptation and deliverance from the evil one.
   1. We are to pray for divine deliverance and guidance.
   2. We are to look to Jesus Christ for help.

3. We are to follow the guidance of the Holy Spirit.
4. We are to remember who we are and maintain our own self-respect.
5. We are to remember those who love and trust us and those whom we love and trust.
6. We have the defense of the Scriptures.
7. We are to put on the whole armor of God.

7
Learning How to Pray

"Lord, teach us to pray" (Luke 11:1).

Principles guiding us in praying the Model Prayer.

1. The fatherhood of God.
2. The brotherhood of all believers.
3. The holiness or sacredness of God demanding reverence and respect.
4. The lordship of Jesus.
5. God's loving purpose and desire.
6. Dependence upon God to supply our physical needs.
7. Dependence on God to supply our spiritual needs.
8. God's guidance and protection.
9. "For thine is the kingdom . . . power . . . and glory forever."

8
God Answers Prayer

"If you then, who are evil, who know to give good gifts to your children, how much more will the heavenly Father give the Holy Spirit to those who ask Him!" (Luke 11:13).

I. Need drives us to our Friend.
   1. The embarrassed host in Jesus' parable was in need.
   2. This is a picture of man's spiritual need.
      (1) We have needs which we are unable to fill.

(2) We must be conscious of these needs.

3. The host had a friend to whom he could go.
4. We have a Friend who can supply all our needs.

II. When our need drives us to our Friend, how shall we pray to him?

1. We should go directly to him.
2. We should be frank and specific.
3. We must be persistent.
4. We must have faith in our Friend.

III. The answer to prayer.

1. Jesus says, "Ask, and it will be given you; seek, and you will find; knock and it will be opened to you. For every one that asks receives, and he who seeks finds, and to him who knocks it will be opened."
2. God will do so much more for his children than an earthly father is able to for his own.
3. So, reasons Jesus, the goodness of God is a guarantee to answered prayer.
   (1) If God did not answer prayer, he would be meaner than evil men.
   (2) Therefore his children may ask of him, and he will grant their request.

9
Life as a Prayer

"And he told them a parable, to the effect that they ought always to pray and not lose heart" (Luke 18:1).

I. "They ought always to pray."

1. Does this mean that we are to spend all our time saying our prayers? No.
2. Prayer is an attitude that covers the whole of life.
   (1) Some pray only when in deep need.
   (2) We should pray when all is well also.
   (3) Our attitudes are also prayers.

II. "And not lose heart."

1. Some people faint because they do not pray.
2. Life apart from God always means failure.
3. The world may crucify a praying person, but the cross will spell victory.

III. Jesus told a parable to illustrate this truth of life as a prayer.

1. A widow was in trouble.
   (1) She was seeking legal justice.
   (2) Her case was in the hands of an evil judge.
2. Jesus makes the application.
   (1) God is unlike the wicked judge.
   (2) He will always answer the prayers of his children.

10
Two Sinners Praying

"Two men went up into the temple to pray, one a Pharisee and the other a tax collector" (Luke 18:10).

I. Observe the two men in this parable.

1. The Pharisee
   (1) He was religious.
   (2) He was also morally pure.
   (3) He was honest and just in business deals.
   (4) He was a liberal giver.
2. Now look at the publican or tax collector.
   (1) He had sold out to Rome, the enemy.
   (2) He had been turned out of the synagogue.
   (3) He was ostracized by his own people.
   (4) He was a sinner.

II. Observe their attitude as they pray.

1. Look again at the Pharisee.
2. Notice the attitude of the tax collector.

III. Observe the attitude of Jesus.

1. Jesus condemned the Pharisee.
2. Jesus commended the tax collector.

11
Watching and Praying

"Watch and pray that you may not enter into temptation" (Matt. 26:41).

I. What are we to watch?

1. Ourselves.
   (1) Our thoughts and attitudes.
   (2) Our words.
   (3) Our deeds.
2. We are to watch others also.
   (1) Jesus warned against false prophets.
   (2) We are to watch for good prophets also.
   (3) For opportunities for doing good.
   (4) We are to expect persecution.
3. We are to watch world events.
4. We are to watch for the coming of Jesus.

II. Why are we to watch and pray?

1. Lest we enter into temptation.
2. Lest we be taken by surprise.

III. Observe that praying and watching go together.

1. Unless we pray, our watching will be in the wrong direction.
2. Unless we pray, our watching will be halfhearted and unfruitful.
3. Praying will help us to interpret correctly what we see.
4. Praying will help prepare us for the day when our Lord will return.

12
Conditions of Effective Prayer

"And when you pray . . ." (Matt. 6:5).

I. Jesus stresses the importance of a proper attitude when praying.

1. We must pray in a spirit of reverence.
2. We must have the attitude of humility.
3. The spirit of sincerity must be present.
4. We must have a forgiving spirit whenever we pray.
5. We must have the spirit of gratitude.
6. The right spirit of prayer is the spirit of unselfishness.
7. When we pray we should have the spirit of penitence and deep need.

II. Our prayers should be in the name of Jesus Christ.

1. We must ask for blessings that are in the interest of the Kingdom.
2. Jesus said that if we ask in the name of the Son, God will answer our prayers directly without intercession.

III. We must be in agreement with other Christians about our petitions.

IV. A condition of effective praying is faith in the Lord's answer.

V. All our prayers must be in accordance with God's will.

1. God would not give bad things to his children.
2. The Holy Spirit helps us in our praying and guides us in the right spirit.

VI. We must live in faith in Christ, with his truth in our hearts.

13
Purity and Vision

"Blessed are the pure in heart: for they shall see God" (Matt. 5:8).

I. It is only the pure in heart who shall see God.

1. Who are the pure in heart?
   (1) Those who are morally clean.
   (2) Those who are sincere.
   (3) Those who have no mixed motives.
2. How do we become pure in heart?
   (1) The blood of Jesus cleanses our hearts when we pray sincerely for cleansing.
   (2) By walking in the light and confessing to Jesus, asking him for forgiveness.

II. Jesus said that "the pure in heart shall see God."

1. It does not mean that we shall see God with our natural eyes.
2. Seeing means understanding.

III. In what sense do we see God?

1. We see him in nature.
2. We see him in the lives of true Christians.
3. We see God in the Bible.
4. We see God in history.
5. We see God in the Lord Jesus Christ.

IV. What will enable us to get a clearer vision of God?

1. Single minded devotion and wholehearted love.
2. True faith will enlarge our vision.
3. Worship, prayer, Bible study, love.

14
Christ's Authority in Prayer

"And Jesus came and said to them, 'All authority in heaven and on earth has been given to me'" (Matt. 28:18).

I. Jesus has full authority to hear and answer our prayers.

II. During his ministry Jesus answered many prayers.

1. He changed water to wine at the wedding in Cana.
2. Jesus healed a paralytic man who was lowered through a roof.
3. Jesus cast out an unclean spirit from a man in the synagogue.
4. Jesus raised Jairus's daughter from the dead.
5. Jesus cured a woman of an incurable hemorrhage.
6. Jesus healed an epileptic boy when his disciples had failed out of lack of faith.
7. Jesus restored the slave of a Roman centurion.
8. Jesus removed the demon from the daughter of a Samaritan woman.

III. Jesus sometimes said no to requests that were made out of selfishness and insincerity.

1. He said no to James and John and their ambitious mother.
2. Jesus rebuked his disciples who wished for fire to destroy a village.
3. Jesus denied the request of a covetous man.
4. Jesus turned down the requests of religious authorities who asked him for a sign from heaven.
5. Finally, Jesus will deny the requests of some people on Judgment Day.

15
A Look at Jesus Praying

"As he was praying . . ." (Luke 9:18).

I. He prayed at his baptism.

1. The Holy Spirit came upon him.
2. God spoke and approved this.

II. He prayed during his temptations.

  1. He quoted Scripture to the tempter.
  2. He confirmed that his ministry would be on spiritual lines.

III. He prayed when he dedicated himself to his ministry.

IV. He had the habit of regular prayer.

  1. He went out in some private place to pray.
  2. His disciples heard him praying and asked him to teach them how to pray.
  3. His praying was rewarded—Peter made his great profession as Jesus prayed.

V. He prayed on the Mount of Transfiguration.

VI. He prayed in the presence of death.

VII. God the Father revealed truth to him as he prayed.

VIII. He prayed on the cross.

16
Prayer and Transfiguration

"And he was transfigured before them and his face shone like the sun, and his garments became white as light" (Matt. 17:2).

I. The prayer life of Jesus.

  1. He was a man of prayer.
  2. Luke says, "He went up into the mountain to pray."
  3. What did he pray about?
  4. What happened when he prayed.
  5. True prayer brings a radiant face.

II. His companions on this occasion.

  1. Peter who needed this experience.

2. James who would be the first to lose his life for Jesus.
3. John who was the closest friend to Jesus.
4. Jesus also had some heavenly companions.
   (1) Moses.
   (2) Elijah.
   (3) His Heavenly Father.

III. The meaning of the transfiguration.

1. It showed that Jesus was full of glory and heavenly beauty.
2. It meant victory to Jesus.
3. It meant God's complete approval of his Son.
   (1) It meant much to Jesus.
   (2) It meant much to his disciples.
   (3) It should mean much to you and me.

17
A Prayer for Divine Glory

"Father, the hour has come; glorify thy Son that the Son may glorify thee" (John 17:1).

I. Jesus prays for himself (vv. 1–5).

1. The hour has come, for which he had come into this world.
2. Jesus prays that God will glorify him on the cross and restore him to his Father's side in heaven.

II. Jesus prayed for his disciples (vv. 6–19).

1. He wants them guarded in God's name.
2. He wants them to be one in love, loyalty, and brotherhood.
3. Jesus hopes that his joy might be fulfilled in his disciples.
4. Jesus prays that his disciples may live in and change the world but not be corrupted by it.

5. He wants his disciples to be consecrated to prepare them for their work on earth.

III. Jesus prays for the believers of all ages (vv. 20–26).

1. Jesus prays that we may find unity and love in each other.
2. He prays that all believers be reunited with him in heaven forever.

18
In Gethsemane

"Father, if thou art willing, remove this cup from me; nevertheless not my will, but thine, be done" (Luke 22:42).

I. Jesus observed in his own life what he taught his disciples.

1. That included the doing of God's will in everything.
2. If it included crucifixion, so be it.

II. He came to earth to do God's will whatever that included.

1. It included doing God's work.
2. It was more important than food.
3. It included teaching, preaching, helping, healing.
4. It included crucifixion and suffering.
5. But it also included resurrection and returning to his Father in heaven.

III. Jesus tells us some things that are God's will for us and all people on earth.

1. It is not God's will that any person on earth should perish.
2. It is God's will that every person anywhere should be saved.
3. It is God's will that his Kingdom come on earth.

IV. Jesus saw glorious results brought about by the doing of the Divine will.

   1. Believers become spiritually akin to Jesus and to other Christians.
   2. Doing God's will enables us to understand the teachings of Jesus.

V. The early disciples learned what God's will was, as they listened to Jesus and the Apostles.

19
Prayers from the Cross

I. "Father, forgive them; for they know not what they do" (Luke 23:34).

   1. Jesus believes in the fatherhood of God despite all that has happened.
   2. Even though he was being unjustly crucified, Jesus can still call for the forgiveness of those that were too stupid to realize what they were doing.
   3. Jesus prays that God might lead these people to repentence, revealing his love and generosity.

II. "My God, my God, why hast thou forsaken me?" (Matt. 27:46).

   1. Sin always seeks to bring separation.
   2. This separation must have been doubly horrible for Christ because he had such an intimate relationship with his Father.
   3. The comfort lies in that Jesus endured these hours of separation so that we might never face them.

III. "Father, into thy hands I commit my spirit!" (Luke 23:46).

   1. This is a cry of victory.
   2. We can have the same assurance of victory if we commit our lives to God.

20
Our Great High Priest

"Since then we have a great high priest who has passed through the heavens, Jesus, the Son of God, let us hold fast our confession" (Heb. 4:14).

I. The priest made intercession for himself and the people to God in the Holy of Holies.

  1. When Jesus was crucified, the temple curtain was rent in half, signifying that every man had access to God through Christ.

II. Jesus is our High Priest who provides understanding and sympathy by taking on the sufferings and temptations of mankind.

III. Jesus is faithful to the One that anointed him by fulfilling his duty of missionary and bridge-builder.

IV. God exalted our High Priest to the heavens.

V. Jesus came from the tribe of Judah, a new order, but was appointed by God, making his priesthood last forever.

VI. Jesus made one complete and sufficient sacrifice in atonement for our sins.

VII. Christ is the minister of the sanctuary and the true tabernacle.

VIII. Christ, our High Priest, has obtained eternal redemption for his people by sprinkling his own blood and not the blood of an animal.

IX. We must fix our eyes on our High Priest and do his will.

PART ONE

"Pray as I Say"

1

The God to Whom We Pray

"Pray then like this: Our Father who art in heaven, Hallowed be thy name" (Matt. 6:9).

To what kind of God do we pray? Our conception of God will to a very large extent determine our prayers and indeed our whole life. If we have the right ideas of God, our prayers will be meaningful and availing; but if we have a faulty conception of God, our prayers will be ineffective.

In the Sermon on the Mount Jesus gives us some of his most significant teachings. Here he teaches us how to pray. He pictures the God to whom we pray. Such a God is our heavenly Father. Jesus said, "Pray then like this: Our Father who art in heaven."

This God created all persons, and in that sense he is the Father of all persons, but he is the Father in a special sense of those who have accepted by faith his Son Jesus Christ. Only a Christian can truthfully pray this prayer, for John tells us that Jesus "came to his own home, and his own people received him not. But to all who received him, who believed in his name, he gave power to become children of God; who were born, not of blood nor of the will of the flesh nor of the will of man, but of God" (John 1:11–13). What kind of God is this heavenly Father? Jesus answers that question in this prayer.

First of all, he is the God who lives in heaven: "who art in heaven." Where is heaven? Some think of heaven as located billions of miles away, a place which cannot be seen with the world's most powerful telescope. No living man has located heaven geographically, but that does not prove that heaven does not exist, even geographically. Heaven is where God dwells. God also lives in every believer's heart, for Jesus said, "If a man loves me, he will keep my word, and my Father will love him, and we will come to him and make our home with him" (John 14:23). We receive God by faith, love, obedience, and acceptance of his Son in sincere trust. Heaven is, among other things, a place of beauty, truth, goodness, love, kindness, mercy, righteousness, glory, and eternal life. We live in heaven when God lives in us and we live in God. We need not shout when we pray, for God is nearer than our very breathing. We can whisper a prayer and be heard by him. Heaven is also the eternal home of our soul, where we will dwell forever after we have died and been raised from the dead.

The God to whom we pray is perfect. Jesus said, "You, therefore, must be perfect, as your heavenly Father is perfect" (Matt. 5:48). God is morally perfect. That means that he is sinless, completely without sin. He has never done any wrong. There is absolutely no evil or wickedness in him. He is the criterion of all righteousness and morality. He is perfect in knowledge and wisdom. God has never made a mistake. He has never made an error in judgment or evaluation of character. John wrote, "God is light" (1 John 1:5). That means that in him is perfect knowledge, wisdom, and truth. He is perfect in love. "God is love," wrote the apostle of love (1 John 4:8). Everything about him is lovely, and love is the chief attribute of his character. He manifested that love in the gift of his Son Jesus Christ to be our Savior and Lord.

The God to whom we pray is holy: "Hallowed be thy name." Reverenced and respected be thy very Person. God's name stands for his nature, his deity, his character. He is always to be reverenced. His holiness sets him apart from all others. No other in heaven or on earth, with the exception of Jesus Christ, can be compared with him. He only is the Lord of all. "You shall have no other gods before me" (Exod. 20:3), he declares in his unchanging law. He is the only One worthy of our worship. We are to reverence his name at all times, and that means that we are always to respect everything that is divine. We must never take his name "in vain" (Exod. 20:7). We must never misuse it or show disrespect for it.

The God to whom we pray is a God who knows our needs and provides for them. He feeds the birds, and therefore will feed his children, who are more precious to him than all the birds. His Son said, "Look at the birds of the air: they neither sow nor reap nor gather into barns, and yet your heavenly Father feeds them. Are you not of more value than they?" (Matt. 6:26). He who made the flowers in beautiful colors and forms will care for his children as well. Hear our Lord again:

> Consider the lilies of the field, how they grow; they neither toil nor spin; yet I tell you, even Solomon in all

> his glory was not arrayed like one of these. But if God so clothes the grass of the field, which today is alive and tomorrow is thrown into the oven, will he not much more clothe you, O men of little faith? (Matt. 6:28–30)

You who are to last forever will not be treated like that which lasts for only a day or so.

God knows that we need certain things. "Your Father knows what you need before you ask him," said Jesus (Matt. 6:8). He reminds us again at the close of this lesson on prayer that God knows we need things like food and clothing. Even better than the best earthly father, God will give good things to them that ask him. Listen again to Jesus: "Or what man of you, if his son asks him for bread, will give him a stone? Or if he asks for a fish, will give him a serpent? If you then, who are evil, know how to give good gifts to your children, how much more will your Father who is in heaven give good things to those who ask him!" (Matt. 7:9–11). We need not worry and fret about these essentials, for our Father will provide them. God will be far better to his children than the very best earthly father is to his children. God gives us only good things. Paul wrote to his Christian friends in Philippi, "And my God will supply every need of yours according to his riches in glory in Christ Jesus" (Phil. 4:19).

Again, the God to whom we pray is a God who richly rewards all who serve him. "Your Father who sees in secret will reward you" (Matt. 6:4). Jesus repeats this promise (vv. 6, 18). God sees our almsgiving, our praying, our fasting. We need not parade our virtues or piety before him to remind him of our labors and sacrifices. He sees and understands everything, even our motives and our spirit. He rewards us richly for what we do for him. We are to serve him because we love him and not merely for rewards. However, nothing we do for God, regardless of how small the deed, goes without being rewarded. We shall be repaid a hundredfold. The persecuted Christian will hear him say, "Rejoice and be glad, for your reward is great in heaven" (Matt. 5:12). Every kind deed will receive a reward. Those who have served their fellowmen will hear his word, "Come, O blessed of my Father, inherit the kingdom prepared for you from the foundation of the world" (Matt. 25:34).

Moreover, the God to whom we pray is a forgiving God: "Blessed are the merciful, for they shall obtain mercy" (Matt. 5:7). Jesus said, "For if you forgive men their trespasses, your heavenly Father also will forgive you; but if you do not forgive men their trespasses, neither will your Father forgive your trespasses" (Matt. 6:14, 15). God is merciful and forgiving. The vilest sinner can find mercy from him if that sinner repents and seeks God's pardon. "Unless you repent you will all likewise perish," said Jesus (Luke 13:5). If we have been forgiven, we should be ready and willing and able to forgive others. If we are unmerciful and unforgiving, it is a sign of our own unforgiven condition.

Jesus told a story to illustrate this. A king once had a servant who owed him about ten million dollars, a staggering sum. Since he could not pay this tremendous debt, the king with great generosity completely cancelled it. A fellow servant of this debtor owed him less than twenty dollars, but the debtor demanded immediate payment. The fellow servant asked for mercy, but instead of showing mercy, the deeply indebted servant insisted on immediate payment of this paltry sum. When the king heard of his outrageous conduct, he commanded that the first servant be imprisoned until he should pay his debt of ten million dollars. Having finished the story, Jesus made this comment: "So also my heavenly Father will do to every one of you, if you do not forgive your brother from your heart" (Matt. 18:35).

The God to whom we pray is to be glorified by our living: "Let your light so shine before men, that they may see your good works and give glory to your Father who is in heaven" (Matt. 5:16). The Christian is to reflect the light of Jesus, who is the true light of the world. We send forth the light as we live for him, walking in his truth, showing his spirit of love, witnessing by word and by example for him. Our light is to glorify him and not ourselves. We are to glorify our Lord in all that we say and do.

The God to whom we pray is also the sovereign Lord whose will we are to do. We owe him absolute obedience. His will is the law of our life.

This is the kind of God to whom we pray. Jesus said, "But when you pray, go into your room and shut the door and pray to your Father who is in secret . . ." (Matt. 6:6). Such praying will be meaningful and helpful, a personal and vital communion between a child of God and his loving Father in heaven.

2

The Kingdom of God

"Thy kingdom come" (Matt. 6:10).

Jesus taught his disciples to pray, saying, "Thy kingdom come." This is the first petition in the Lord's Prayer. Every Christian is to pray for the coming of God's kingdom.

Is communism going to win this world? Is God going to be run out of his universe? Is Christianity going to be obliterated? Communism and other "isms" may win some victories, but God's eternal plan and purpose is to establish his kingdom on this earth, or in a new heaven and earth. This physical earth may not even be necessary in God's ultimate purpose. But we are to pray that his kingdom come and his will be done "on earth as it is in heaven." The first burden of our praying is to be for the coming of the kingdom of God.

Now what is the kingdom of God? It is the realm in and over which God reigns in the hearts of persons who accept his Son Jesus Christ as Savior and Lord and who seek always to do the divine will in the relationships of life. The kingdom of God and Christ's kingdom are identical. The kingdom is primarily spiritual, not material. That means that it is in the hearts of persons. It is not a political or military kingdom like the Jews were looking for in the first century and before. Jesus said, "The kingdom of God is not coming with signs to be observed; nor will they say, 'Lo, here it is!' or 'There!' for behold, the kingdom of God is in the midst of you" (Luke 17:20, 21). One can have the kingdom in his heart and live in Russia or Red China. I am confident that there are many members of God's spiritual kingdom in both of those countries as well as in other communist nations. Paul describes the kingdom in spiritual terms: "For the kingdom of God does not mean food and drink but righteousness and peace and joy in the Holy Spirit" (Rom. 14:17). The kingdom of God and the kingdom of heaven are the same, and both terms are used interchangeably in the Gospels.

The kingdom of God is universal in scope and purpose, having no racial or national or geographical boundaries. It is heavenly in origin. Our Lord said to Pilate: "My kingship is not of this world; if my kingship were of this world, my servants would fight, that I might not be handed over to the Jews; but my kingship is not from the world" (John 18:36). But it does come down from heaven to earth. In his vision John heard voices in heaven, saying, "The kingdom of the world has become the kingdom of our Lord and of his Christ, and he shall reign for ever and ever" (Rev. 11:15). That prophecy is still to be fulfilled.

The kingdom will, however, have outward manifestations. It will affect governments, social and political conditions, and all life on this earth. As it comes nearer, these earthly conditions will improve, and those who accept Christ as King will strive to obey and please him in all their relationships. God's kingdom will one day supersede earthly governments. The present age will pass away, and the new age of God's reign will come.

Now let us consider the coming of God's kingdom. What about the time of its coming? In one sense it has already come. John the Baptist said, "Repent, for the kingdom of heaven is at hand" (Matt. 3:2). Jesus also began to preach, saying, "Repent, for the kingdom of heaven is at hand" (Matt. 4:17). The kingdom is also now in the process of coming. It comes anytime a person lets the King enter his heart and control his life. But it also comes in the future, when it is fully established in the hearts of believers everywhere.

How does the kingdom come? Its coming may be gradual and quiet. Jesus said, "The kingdom of God is as if a man should scatter seed upon the ground, and should sleep and rise night and day, and the seed should sprout and grow, he knows not how. The earth produces of itself, first the blade, then the ear, then the full grain in the ear" (Mark 4:26–28). The parable of the mustard seed and the parable of the leaven teach this same truth. On the other hand, the kingdom of God sometimes comes suddenly and catastrophically. Our Lord said: "For as the lightning comes from the east and shines as far as the west, so will be the coming of the Son of man" (Matt. 24:27). It will come fully when Jesus returns to earth. He will gather his redeemed into his eternal kingdom.

What are we to do about bringing in the kingdom? Well, we are to pray for its coming, as Jesus plainly teaches here. And if we pray, we shall also work and witness to others about the King, seeking to bring them into his kingdom. We are to recognize the fact that the kingdom is God's free gift. Our Lord said to his disciples: "Fear not, little flock, for it is your Father's good pleasure to give you the kingdom" (Luke 12:32). We are to make it the supreme object of our lives. "But seek first his kingdom and his righteousness," said Jesus, "and all these things shall be yours as well" (Matt. 6:33). Finding the kingdom is like finding a hidden treasure in a field. We go and sell our other possessions in order to buy that field. It is like the dealer in pearls who finds a priceless pearl and sells his other pearls to get this one jewel. Jesus says in these parables that the kingdom of God is worth the sacrifice of all other things. Our first aim in life should be to find this kingdom and enter it.

God's kingdom is, and it is growing. It grows extensively, like the mustard seed which is very small but when grown produces a large plant. The kingdom had small beginnings in a stable in Bethlehem, but now it covers large portions of the earth. It grows intensively, like the leaven that permeates the whole loaf. The kingdom works from within and spreads to every part of one's life and to other lives in a chain reaction. The true kingdom will continue to spread and expand until all that it touches is transformed and brought into the kingdom.

God is the King of the kingdom. He rules through Christ our Lord, who is also called the King. Many Old Testament passages speak of the coming King, the Messiah. He is to have an eternal kingdom. He is to sit upon the throne of David and reign forever. Jesus came as the King. The "wise men from the East came to Jerusalem, saying, 'Where is he who has been born king of the Jews? For we have seen his star in the East, and have come to worship him'" (Matt. 2:1, 2). Later the people shouted, "Blessed is the King who comes in the name of the Lord! Peace in heaven and glory in the highest!" (Luke 19:38).

But who are the subjects or citizens in God's kingdom? Some cannot enter it as they are. Those who have never had a spiritual birth through the work of the Holy Spirit in their heart are kept from entering this spiritual kingdom. The King himself said, "Truly, truly, I say to you, unless one is born of water and the Spirit, he cannot enter the kingdom of God" (John 3:5). This spiritual birth takes place when one repents of sin and believes in Christ as Savior and Lord. The hypocrite cannot enter. Jesus said, "For I tell you, unless your righteousness exceeds that of the scribes and Pharisees, you will never enter the kingdom of heaven" (Matt. 5:20). That means that we must have more than an outward respectability. We must have an inward righteousness that comes from a transformed heart and mind. We must have the sort of righteousness that comes through faith in Christ who is our righteousness.

The proud and arrogant cannot enter. Our Lord said, "Truly, I say to you, unless you turn and become like children, you will never enter the kingdom of heaven" (Matt. 18:3). We enter by the door of humility. The apostle Paul gave a long list of those who can never enter unless they repent. "Do you not know that the unrighteous will not inherit the kingdom of God? Do not be deceived; neither the immoral, nor idolaters, nor adulterers, nor homosexuals, nor thieves, nor the greedy, nor drunkards, nor revilers, nor robbers will inherit the kingdom of God. And such were some of you. But you were washed, you were sanctified, you were justified in the name of the Lord Jesus Christ and in the Spirit of our God" (1 Cor. 6:9–11).

Again, Paul wrote very clearly:

> Now the works of the flesh are plain: immorality, impurity, licentiousness, idolatry, sorcery, enmity, strife, jealousy, anger, selfishness, dissension, party spirit, envy, drunkenness, carousing, and the like. I warn you, as I warned you before, that those who do such things shall not inherit the kingdom of God. (Gal. 5:19–21)

The person who trusts in his riches cannot enter God's kingdom. "How hard it is," declared our Master, "for those who have riches to enter the kingdom of God! For it is easier for a camel to go through the eye of a needle than for a rich man to enter the kingdom of God" (Luke 18:24, 25). The rich man, like the poor man, must come in by trusting in the King, not in his wealth.

But many will enter. We can say that all who are born again by the Holy Spirit will enter (John 3:3), for they must repent and believe before this spiritual experience can occur. Those who do God's will shall enter, for the Lord said: "Not every one who says to me, 'Lord, Lord,' shall enter the kingdom of heaven, but he who does the will of my Father who is in heaven" (Matt. 7:21). The poor in spirit and the humble will enter, for Jesus said, "Blessed are the poor in spirit, for theirs is the kingdom of heaven" (Matt. 5:3). Those who sincerely serve Christ by serving the needy will find their way into the kingdom:

> Then the King will say to those at his right hand, 'Come, O blessed of my Father, inherit the kingdom

> prepared for you from the foundation of the world; for I was hungry and you gave me food, I was thirsty and you gave me drink, I was a stranger and you welcomed me, I was naked and you clothed me, I was sick and you visited me'. . . And the King will answer them, 'Truly, I say to you, as you did it to one of the least of these my brethren, you did it to me' (Matt. 25: 34–35, 40)

Everyone who has had the opportunity of submitting voluntarily to Jesus Christ and has done so in childlike faith and humility will be in the kingdom. In fact, he is already in it, and will be in it when the King comes and reigns forevermore.

Some will be great in the kingdom. Those who have obeyed and taught the King's commandments will occupy positions of greatness (Matt. 5:19). Those who have childlike humility and feel most unworthy will find themselves in high places. The King said, "Whoever humbles himself like this child, he is the greatest in the kingdom of heaven" (Matt. 18:4). Service is the test of greatness: "He who is greatest among you shall be your servant" (Matt. 23:11).

We are to pray, "Thy kingdom come." We are to make it our first aim to enter this kingdom. And then we are to seek to bring others into it. Jesus told the parable of the tares (Matt. 13:24–30) and explained its meaning.

> Just as the weeds are gathered and burned with fire, so will it be at the close of the age. The Son of man will send his angels, and they will gather out of his kingdom all causes of sin and all evildoers, and throw them into the furnace of fire; there men will weep and gnash their teeth. Then the righteous will shine like the sun in the kingdom of their Father. (vv. 40–43)

3

The Will of God

"Thy will be done, On earth as it is in heaven" (Matt. 6:10).

Jesus taught his disciples to pray, saying, "Our Father who art in heaven, Hallowed be thy name. Thy kingdom come, Thy will be done, On earth as it is in heaven" (Matt. 6:9, 10). God's will is to be done on earth just as it is done in heaven. Life is a matter of obedience to someone's will: our own will, the will of some other person, the will of God, or the will of Satan. The Christian is to seek to make his will conform to God's will. A perceptive preacher has declared that prayer may change God's action, but it does not change his intention. He meant that God's intention, his will, is always right, but what he does depends on man's cooperation with him. Is God's will being done in our lives today?

We can see that Jesus, God's Son, lived by God's will perfectly. That was his law of life. He sought to know and to do God's will. He said, "I can do nothing on my own authority; as I hear, I judge; and my judgment is just, because I seek not my own will but the will of him who sent me" (John 5:30). He sought to know God's will by studying the Scriptures and by praying. He came to earth to do God's will. He said so precisely. "For I have come down from heaven, not to do my own will, but the will of him who sent me" (John 6:38). The verses that follow show how thoroughly he understood God's will and was ready to carry it out fully. His life was unselfish and God-centered. He said to his disciples by Jacob's well in Samaria, "My food is to do the will of him who sent me, and to accomplish his work" (John 4:34). This is what sustained him and gave purpose to his life.

Fear of death did not turn him aside. Satan tried to get him to change his will and avoid the cross, offering him "all the kingdoms of the world and the glory of them" (Matt. 4:8). But Jesus rebuked him. Later Jesus prayed, "Father, if thou art willing, remove this cup from me; nevertheless not my will, but thine, be done" (Luke 22:42). The word "nevertheless" made all the difference. Doing God's will cost him suffering and death upon the cross, but he was willing to pay this price for man's redemption from sin.

By doing God's will he won a great victory. He provided for our salvation upon the cross. It is in his blood that we have our redemption from sin. His cross was followed by his crown. Because he was obedient to death, God highly exalted him and gave him the supreme name. Before him shall every knee bow in recognition of his right to be the supreme Ruler of the universe.

But what is God's will for us? How can we know the answer to that? To know his will is to know his desire and purpose for us: what he wants us to be and do. His will is always the right thing, always best for us. God's will is always in keeping with his character. He is holy, just, righteous, and loving. He never wills what is evil or wrong, for to do so would contradict his very nature as God.

The Bible tells us some things about God's will. It is his will, his desire, that all persons be saved. Paul wrote to Timothy, saying, "This is good, and it is acceptable in the sight of God our Savior, who desires all men to be saved and to come to the knowledge of the truth" (1 Tim. 2:3, 4). Peter wrote that God "is forbearing toward you, not wishing that any should perish, but that all should reach repentance" (2 Peter 3:9). If we come to genuine repentance we shall come to eternal life in the kingdom. Our Lord assures us, "So it is not the will of my Father who is in heaven that one of these little ones should perish" (Matt. 18:14). God wants every man, woman, and child in the whole world to be saved. He has done everything in his power to save all. If anyone is lost, it is because that person insists on doing his own will rather than God's. Jesus wept over the sinful city. "O Jerusalem, Jerusalem, killing the prophets and stoning those who are sent to you! How often would I have gathered your children together as a hen gathers her brood under her wings, and you would not!" (Luke 13:34). We must say to God, "Thy will be done," or God will say to us, "Your own will be done." He said, "I would . . . and you would not!" There was a clash of wills. Only our own stubborn rebellion as we insist on having our own way can keep God from saving us.

It is God's will that we keep his commandments. He would not have given them to us if he had not intended for us to keep them. The commandments are summed up in our love for God and man. These are the first and second commandments, or the first and one like it, and Jesus said, "On these two commandments depend all the law and the prophets" (Matt. 22:40).

It is God's will that we obey his Son, Jesus Christ, that we believe on him, follow him, honor him, love him, and live by his teachings. In John 3:36 we read, "He who believes in the Son has eternal life; he who does not obey the Son shall not see life, but the wrath of God rests upon him."

We can discover God's will by prayer and Bible study. Jesus said, "My teaching is not mine, but his who sent me; if any man's will is to do his will, he shall know whether the teaching is from God or whether I am speaking on my own authority" (John 7:16, 17). If we genuinely desire to know, we can discover that the teachings of Jesus carry out God's will by prayerful study of the Bible and by our own willingness to obey him. We shall be able to recognize God's will when we see it.

But some difficult questions arise concerning God's will, questions we cannot hastily brush aside:

Is war ever his will? God does not desire war. He takes no delight in it. But he sometimes permits it for it is brought on by man's rebellion against the will of God. It is God's will that truth, justice, and righteousness prevail. It is sometimes necessary to defend ourselves and our loved ones against tyrants and lawless men who would destroy us and the things in our world. We should not be blind to the obvious fact that there are those in this world, even some in our own nation, who would if they could completely destroy us and our way of life. They would eliminate us and all that we cherish.

They have openly declared this as their intention. It would be extreme folly not to prepare to resist such persons and forces. We should remind ourselves, however, that we can resist, not only by military power, but also by living in truth and righteousness and by seeking to bring the kingdom of God on earth. This petition, "Thy will be done," is very closely linked with "Thy kingdom come." The kingdom will come only as God's will is done on earth as it is in heaven.

Is suffering God's will? It is not his wish that we suffer. He takes no delight in our pains. Jesus healed the sick and relieved the oppressed. He would not have spent so much time and energy doing this if he had believed suffering in itself is a blessing. God permits suffering and pain. Pain may be, and often is, a warning that leads us to do something to prevent further suffering or death. We can also use necessary sufferings to glorify God. Many people never would have discovered God and his way if the suffering caused by following their own way had not brought them to attention. We can say it is better to suffer than to do evil or fail to do God's will. That is why Jesus went to the cross. That is why martyrs have given their lives for righteousness' sake.

Is death God's will? God has no delight in the death of the wicked. He takes no delight in the death of innocent victims of sin and crime, accident and disease. We are wrong when we say of death, "It was the Lord's will." That may sound pious, but the truth is that God does not desire our death, and he did something to defeat it. Death often comes as the result of disobedience and disregard for God's laws and his will. But our physical death can often be a blessing. What if the old worn-out body had to continue in pain unable to die?

Can you imagine what the world would be like if all the people who had ever lived were still on earth even though they had grown old, feeble, and completely helpless? Many things are far worse than death: for example, betraying or denying the Lord.

I believe that we can know without a doubt what God's will is if we honestly and eagerly seek it, and if we let the Holy Spirit guide us. We can even advance a step farther and ask, What are the results of doing God's will? What are the benefits and rewards?

The most important result is that we enter the kingdom of God. Jesus said, "Not every one who says to me, 'Lord, Lord,' shall enter the kingdom of heaven, but he who does the will of my Father who is in heaven" (Matt. 7:21). It is through obedience to God that we enter. We have eternal life in the kingdom. John wrote, "And the world passes away, and the lust of it; but he who does the will of God abides for ever" (1 John 2:17).

We develop a spiritual kinship with Jesus by doing God's will. "For whoever does the will of my Father in heaven is my brother, and sister, and mother" (Matt. 12:50). We have this wonderful purpose for living. Some people can see no meaning in life, but the Christian lives to please God. We may have to suffer, but our sufferings make it possible for God to bless us in special ways. We shall receive the crown of life one day. Those who suffer persecution for righteousness' sake will have a great reward (Matt. 5:12).

Another reward for doing God's will is having our lives become a blessing to others. Doing God's will makes us unselfish and loving toward others. It leads us to witness, to heal the sick, and to minister to the needy. God will make our lives a blessing if only we do his will.

Are we ready to pray this prayer: "Thy will be done, On earth as it is in heaven"? It is done perfectly in heaven. Our prayer should be that it be done perfectly on earth also.

May we let God's will be done in all of life, in our personal relationships, in our social activities, in our homelife, in our church life, and in our business and professional life.

It is God's will for us to be Christians. If we are not already Christians, we may become such right now by yielding our own will to Christ's will, by saying yes to God's Son who died on the cross to save us from sin.

It is God's will that every Christian be a good member of the church of the Lord. If you are not one now, you may become one by turning to the Lord and resolving to be faithful and loyal to him in his church.

It is God's will that we live for his glory. He will help us do that if that is our earnest desire and unswerving purpose. And so we pray: "Our Father who art in heaven, Hallowed be thy name. Thy kingdom come, Thy will be done, On earth as it is in heaven."

4

Our Daily Bread

"Give us this day our daily bread" (Matt. 6:11).

Man does not live by bread alone, but without bread he cannot live at all. "Bread" here is a symbol for what is essential to physical life, especially food. Bread is "the staff of life," undergirding all our material needs. People in the days of Jesus were asking, "What shall we eat? . . . What shall we drink? . . . What shall we wear?" (Matt. 6:31). We ask the same questions today. The supply of food has always been a problem. Even in our time of scientific production, much of the world is hungry. In fact, most people are undernourished, while some are grossly overfed.

Jesus recognized this problem and dealt with it. He performed miracles to feed the hungry. He was vitally concerned with the health and happiness of the people. The Lord's Prayer teaches us to pray about this problem: "Give us this day our daily bread." This petition is full of meaning and significance.

To begin with, we should observe that while

bread is important, some things come before bread in importance.

God comes first. We are to pray, saying, "Our Father, who art in heaven." He is the One without whom all else is useless and meaningless. We must put God before parents, children, wife, husband, brothers, sisters, neighbors. We must love him more than any other. His name comes first: "Hallowed be thy name." We are to put his sacred name and his cause before business, pleasure, family, food. We are not to profane his name in getting food or material things.

His kingdom comes before bread. The first petition in the Lord's Prayer is, "Thy kingdom come," and Jesus said, "But seek first his kingdom and his righteousness, and all these things shall be yours as well" (Matt. 6:33). His kingdom is the "pearl of great price," worth the sacrifice of all other pearls. It is the discovered treasure that is worth more than all other treasures. If we put his kingdom first, material things will take a secondary place, but they will be added. God's reign in our lives is more important than food, or anything else.

God's will comes before bread: "Thy will be done." We are to live by his will, even if we must go hungry. The devil tried to get Jesus to put food before God's will by turning stones into bread, but our Lord answered, "It is written, 'Man shall not live by bread alone, but by every word that proceeds from the mouth of God'" (Matt. 4:4).

We should always remind ourselves that we are dependent upon God to supply our bread. This petition for bread is addressed to God, the Creator and Owner of all things. He has provided food aplenty. We can say with the prodigal son, "How many of my father's hired servants have bread enough and to spare" (Luke 15:17).

Think of the marvelous variety and quantity of food in the world. There is food for every kind of appetite, something to satisfy every taste. All this food belongs to God. He created it and caused it to grow. Many wonderful things have been done by man, but man has never made a synthetic seed that would grow and reproduce.

How are we to get food for our bodies? Some steal it. They rob, plunder, and even murder, to get it. Some grab it from God's garden as if it belonged to them. They waste it, withhold it from others, never thank God for it, and fail to recognize him as the giver of it. Someone has pictured them as like pigs under the oak tree eating acorns and never looking up to see where they came from. We are to ask God for food, "Give us this day our daily bread." We are to thankfully acknowledge him as the Owner upon whom we are completely dependent. "Ask, and it will be given you," said Jesus (Matt. 7:7). He went on to say, "Or what man of you, if his son asks him for bread, will give him a stone? Or if he asks for a fish, will give him a serpent? If you then, who are evil, know how to give good gifts to your children, how much more will your Father who is in heaven give good things to those who ask him!" (Matt. 7:9–11). God has always provided for his own. He gave manna and quail from heaven and water from the rock when his people were hungry and thirsty in the wilderness. James wrote, "You do not have, because you do not ask. You ask and do not receive, because you ask wrongly, to spend it on your passions" (James 4:2, 3).

Not only are we to ask God for food, but we are to work for it. God provides food, but he does not serve breakfast in bed on a silver platter. We are commanded to work and earn our bread. This prayer is not for a lazy person who wants to avoid work. Paul told some in the early church that if a man would not work neither should he be fed.

We are to work and to trust God to supply our needs. We are not to be filled with anxiety about them. Listen to the Lord: "Therefore I tell you, do not be anxious about your life, what you shall eat or what you shall drink, nor about your body, what you shall put on. Is not life more than food, and the body more than clothing?" (Matt. 6:25). Life does not consist in an abundance of food and clothing or material things. Jesus pointed to the birds as the objects of God's loving care. They are not anxious or bothered, and yet God feeds them. He pointed to the lovely flowers, and said that God who clothes them so richly would not neglect his own children. Man is valued in God's sight and this is an assurance that he will provide for our needs. Jesus teaches that excess worry about our daily bread is mistrustful, useless, unreasonable, and pagan. God will provide for our needs if we seek his kingdom first and trust him.

Some are so anxious that they seek to hoard food in abundance for the future. They act like the rich fool in the parable. They tear down their small barns and build larger ones to store away their grain and their goods, saying, "Soul, you have ample goods laid up for many years" (Luke 12:19). But God says that they are playing the fool. When God provided manna in the wilderness, the children of Israel had to gather it daily, except on the sabbath day (Exod. 16:5, 27). They could not hoard it, lest it spoil. So we are to pray for our daily bread, enough for a day at a time. Jesus does not condemn foresight, but he does condemn undue anxiety about our daily bread and our material needs.

This petition also forbids selfish praying for bread. "Give us this day our daily bread." Note carefully the plural "us" and "our." This means that we must recognize the needs and rights of others for bread. Hungry people will fight, wage war, hurl atomic bombs, if they do not get their daily bread. We cannot ignore a hungry world. We have shared and are sharing. We are to help feed the world, not for political reasons, but because it is right and Christlike to do so.

Jesus forbids us to live selfishly. We must live as brothers in one family, sharing our bread with one another. To ignore our brother's need is to commit spiritual suicide. To meet that need is to discover Christ. To feed the hungry is to feed the One who said, "I was hungry and you gave me food. . . . Truly, I say to you, as you did it to one of the least of these my brethren, you did it to me" (Matt. 25:35, 40). "Give to him who begs from you, and do not refuse him who would borrow from you" said Jesus (Matt. 5:42). He did not say that we are to give exactly what he asks for, but we are to give something that will help to supply his basic needs.

This petition in the Lord's prayer has a profound echo in Jesus' telling us that he is "the bread of life" (John 6:35). "Do not labor for the food which perishes, but for the food which endures to eternal life, which the Son of man will give to you" (v. 27). "Truly, truly, I say to you, it was not Moses who gave you the bread from heaven; my Father gives you the true bread from heaven" (v. 32). As bread is necessary for the body, so this spiritual bread is necessary for the soul. If we eat of this spiritual bread we shall live forever (v. 58).

How do we partake of the "bread of life?" By coming in childlike faith to Jesus, committing our lives to him, yielding ourselves in trustful obedience, by walking daily with him by faith. Then we shall be seeking first his kingdom and his righteousness. Then he will not only give us bread for the body but will feed our souls with the bread of life. Jesus said, "To him who conquers I will grant to eat of the tree of life, which is in the Paradise of God" (Rev. 2:7). If we wash our robes in the blood of the Lamb, we shall have the right to the tree of life and eat and live forever.

God says to a spiritually hungry world today:

> Ho, every one who thirsts, come to the waters; and he who has no money, come, buy and eat! Come, buy wine and milk without money and without price. Why do you spend your money for that which is not bread, and your labor for that which does not satisfy? Hearken diligently to me, and eat what is good, and delight yourselves in fatness. Incline your ear, and come to me; hear, that your soul may live. (Isa. 55:1–3)

"Give us this day our daily bread." Give us bread for the body and, even more, bread for the soul!

5

Forgiveness of Sins

"And forgive us our debts, As we also have forgiven our debtors . . . . For if you forgive men their trespasses, your heavenly Father also will forgive you; but if you do not forgive men their trespasses, neither will your Father forgive your trespasses" (Matt. 6:12, 14, 15).

In our praying we are to remember the God to whom we pray. We are to put his name, his kingdom, and his will first, before everything else. His name is to be reverenced on earth as it is in heaven. His kingdom is to come on earth as it has come in heaven. His will is to be done on earth here and now just as it is done in heaven. After putting these spiritual things first, we are to think of our own needs and pray for our daily bread. But there is another crucial need, forgiveness. Bread comes before forgiveness only because without bread there would be no life. Now we consider the next petition in the Lord's prayer: "And forgive us our debts, As we also have forgiven our debtors."

We need to pray this prayer for divine forgiveness for many reasons.

First, because we have all sinned. The Bible declares this truth, "All have sinned and fall short of the glory of God" (Rom. 3:23). We have sinned in the past, and we continue in the present to fall short of God's glory. John wrote: "If we say we have not sinned, we make him a liar, and his word is not in us" (1 John 1:10). What is sin? The New Testament answer to this question makes it quite obvious that we are all guilty.

Sins are referred to as our debts. We owe God certain obligations. We owe it to him to live according to his plan and purpose, to obey and please him in everything. We are obligated to God because he gave us life and all things we enjoy in this world. We owe him everything we have, because we have received everything from him. We have never created anything. Everything is the gift of God.

Trespasses are sins. To trespass is to transgress, or to go beyond what is permitted. It is to get out of bounds, off-limits. It is to step over onto the wrong side. That surely makes each and everyone guilty. We have turned aside from God's way and have walked in our own selfish way. Isaiah wrote centuries before Christ came, "All we like sheep have gone astray; we have turned every one to his own way" (Isa. 53:6). One who claims that he has never missed the mark is a conceited hypocrite and is guilty of one of the worst of sins—the sin of spiritual pride.

Sin is lawlessness, a violation of God's law. We sometimes speak of breaking God's laws, but we cannot actually do that. We only break ourselves against his divine laws, and in doing so we confirm his law. We keep the law of God when we love him with our whole being and love our neighbor as ourself. Does any one of us claim that we have always done that?

Another word for sin is "unrighteousness," the failure to measure up to God's standard. Our righteousness is described in the Bible as a filthy garment: "We have all become like one who is unclean, and all our righteous deeds are like a polluted garment" (Isa. 64:6). That is how our righteousness appears when contrasted with the perfect righteousness of Jesus Christ.

Sin is iniquity, or moral crookedness, perverseness. Instead of walking the straight way, our path often looks like that of the snake or the drunken man who reels and staggers from side to side.

Forty times or more in the New Testament Jesus used a word for sin that is translated "evil." Sin has its origin in the evil one. It is wickedness, devilishness, wrongdoing. Seven different Greek words are used in the New Testament for "sin." And we are guilty of all seven descriptions or definitions of sin.

The Bible speaks of the sin of unbelief, the major sin. It describes sins of the disposition, sins of the flesh, sins of omission, and sins of commission.

We might define a sin as any voluntary thought, word, attitude, or act that is contrary to God's will. In this sense Jesus Christ was the only person who was without sin—with the exception of babies and children too immature to know the difference between right and wrong and persons with mental conditions which make them not responsible for their thoughts, words, and acts. We should pray for forgiveness because we have all sinned and continue to sin, falling short of God's standard and glory.

We should pray for forgiveness because of what unforgiveness means. Unforgiven sinners become slaves to sin. Jesus is our authority—there can be no higher authority: "Truly, truly, I say to you, every one who commits sin is a slave to sin" (John 8:34). He is talking about the habit of sinning. This is clear from the Greek tense used here. The devil takes us captive when we habitually commit sin. Sin brings misery, heartache, and suffering. It always leads to wretchedness and never to true happiness. It is very deceitful, promising joy but paying in misery. It produces wretchedness in the heart of the sinner and in the lives of those whom he sins against. Sin breaks fellowship, disrupts families, and destroys character. Unforgiven sin leads to spiritual death and eternal ruin. The Bible says, "For the wages of sin is death" (Rom. 6:23). James tells us, "Then desire when it has conceived gives birth to sin; and sin when it is full-grown brings forth death" (James 1:15). And John says, "He who does not obey the Son shall not see life, but the wrath of God rests upon him" (John 3:36). Unforgiven sinners according to the Bible "perish," are "condemned," are "lost," and are "cast into hell."

We need to pray this prayer because of what forgiveness does. God's forgiveness cleanses us of sin. Sin is erased from the record, cancelled, forgotten, buried in the depth of the sea. Forgiveness restores us to a right relationship with God, changing our hostility to love, our disobedience to obedience, our greed to generosity. It makes us new persons in Christ through a spiritual birth from above. It assures us of eternal life and salvation and heaven. It changes our attitude and relationship to our fellowmen. We are able to love our fellowmen and seek their highest welfare.

What must we do to get this divine forgiveness?

We must repent and confess our sins. David committed horrible sins. When he tried to hide his sins, he was miserable and felt estranged from God. He wrote: "When I declared not my sin, my body wasted away through my groaning all day long. For day and night thy hand was heavy upon me; my strength was dried up as by the heat of summer" (Ps. 32:3, 4). But things changed when he confessed his sin to God. "I acknowledged my sin to thee, and I did not hide my iniquity; I said, 'I will confess my transgressions to the Lord'; then thou didst forgive the guilt of my sin" (v. 5). In First John we read, "If we confess our sins, he is faithful and just, and will forgive our sins and cleanse us from all unrighteousness" (1:9). To repent means to change one's mind or attitude and conduct. One must change his attitude about sin, turn away from it, stop practicing it.

To obtain forgiveness we must believe on Jesus Christ who has made atonement for our sins. God forgives through his Son. The New Testament presents Jesus as the only remedy for sin. John the Baptist said, "Behold, the Lamb of God, who takes away the sin of the world!" (John 1:29). Jesus at the Last Supper said to his disciples as he offered them the cup of wine: "Drink of it, all of you; for this is my blood of the covenant, which is poured out for many for the forgiveness of sins" (Matt. 26:27, 28). The risen Christ said to his disciples, "Thus it is written, that the Christ should suffer and on the third day rise from the dead, and that repentance and forgiveness of sins should be preached in his name to all nations" (Luke 24:46, 47). The apostle Paul declared the gospel of the Son of God's love "in whom we have redemption, the forgiveness of sins" (Col. 1:14). The beloved disciple wrote: "If we walk in the light, as he is in the light, we have fellowship with one another, and the blood of Jesus his Son cleanses us from all sin" (1 John 1:7). It is our faith in Jesus that enables us to receive divine forgiveness, as John tells us:

> For God so loved the world that he gave his only Son, that whoever believes in him should not perish but have eternal life. For God sent the Son into the world, not to condemn the world, but that the world might be saved through him. He who believes in him is not condemned; he who does not believe is condemned already, because he has not believed in the name of the only Son of God. (John 3:16–18)

Jesus said, "I told you that you would die in your sins, for you will die in your sins unless you believe that I am he" (John 8:24).

Not only must we repent, confess, and believe, but we must forgive. That means to be forgiving in attitude and action toward others if we expect to receive divine forgiveness. We pray, "Forgive us . . . *As* we also have forgiven." That means we are asking God to treat us as we treat others in this matter of forgiveness, to forgive us to the extent that we forgive our friends and our family members. Jesus makes an unambiguous comment on this petition: "For if you forgive men their trespasses, your heavenly Father also will forgive you; but if you do not forgive men their trespasses, neither will your Father forgive your trespasses" (Matt. 6:14, 15). Paul wrote: "And be kind to one another, tenderhearted, forgiving one another, as God in Christ forgave you" (Eph. 4:32).

Jesus told Simon Peter to be willing to forgive a brother who sinned against him "seventy times seven" times, or indefinitely. Then he told his disciples of the servant who owed his master the equivalent of about ten million dollars, which he could not pay. At first the wealthy master ordered him and his family to be sold, along with his possessions, so that payment could be made. When the servant earnestly begged for mercy and promised to pay, his master with kingly generosity cancelled the entire debt. Instead of being kind and grateful and generous like his master, this scoundrel went out and found one of his fellow servants who owed him a paltry sum, less than twenty dollars. He demanded immediate payment. His fellow servant begged for mercy, but this rascal refused to show any mercy and had his fellow servant thrown into debtors' prison. When this became known, the master of this unmerciful servant exploded in wrath: "You wicked servant! I forgave you all that debt because you besought me; and should not you have had mercy on your fellow servant, as I had mercy on you?" (Matt. 18:32, 33). So his master had him cast into prison until he should pay the ten million dollars. What a meaningful parable! Notice carefully the comment of Jesus: "So also my heavenly Father will do to every one of you, if you do not forgive your brother from your heart" (v. 35). In the matter of forgiveness God will treat us as we treat others. In one of the beatitudes Jesus said, "Blessed are the merciful, for they shall obtain mercy" (Matt. 5:7). Again, he had said in his Sermon on the Mount, "The measure you give will be the measure you get" (Matt. 7:2).

To pray sincerely the prayer of our Lord means that we do receive forgiveness. God had said long ago through Isaiah his prophet: "Come now, let us reason together, says the Lord: though your sins are like scarlet, they shall be as white as snow; though they are red like crimson, they shall become like wool" (Isa. 1:18). Isaiah wrote: "Seek the Lord while he may be found, call upon him while he is near; let the wicked forsake his way, and the unrighteous man his thoughts; let him return to the Lord, that he may have mercy on him, and to our God, for he will abundantly pardon" (Isa. 55:6, 7). If we come to Jesus confessing our sins and believing on him, he will say to us, "Neither do I condemn you; go, and do not sin again" (John 8:11).

Jesus Christ has the power and the authority to forgive sins. Recall the narrative of the paralytic to whom Jesus said, "Take heart, my son; your sins are forgiven" (Matt. 9:2). Jesus demonstrated his authority on earth to forgive sins by healing this paralytic immediately. Any Christian has the power and the authority from his Lord to declare a person's sins forgiven when that person genuinely repents and believes on Jesus Christ, thus meeting the conditions of divine forgiveness.

The angel of the Lord told Joseph that Mary would bear a son, "And you shall call his name Jesus, for he will save his people from their sins" (Matt. 1:21). Jesus Christ, God's beloved Son, came into the world that men might find forgiveness for their sins. We can find forgiveness for our sins in Christ alone, who taught us to pray: "And forgive us our debts, as we also have forgiven our debtors."

6

God's Guidance and Deliverance

"And lead us not into temptation, But deliver us from evil" (Matt. 6:13).

When we come to the end of a year we do not know what the new year will bring us. Only God knows. But we do know one thing: it will bring temptation, and the devil will still be seeking to lure us into sin. We will need guidance and deliverance from evil. We will need to stand against the wiles of the devil. Our warfare is against evil forces. Paul reminds us of this fact: "For we are not contending against flesh and blood, but against the principalities, against the powers, against the world rulers of this present darkness, against the spiritual hosts of wickedness in the heavenly places" (Eph. 6:12). Jesus teaches us to pray for guidance and deliverance.

We need to examine the origin and nature of temptation. We are to pray, "And lead us not into temptation." Surely God would not lead anyone to do evil. A gracious

God never seeks to entice us into sin. James, the Lord's brother, wrote in the New Testament, "Let no one say when he is tempted, 'I am tempted of God'; for God cannot be tempted with evil and he himself tempts no one" (James 1:13).

God permits us to be tempted. The word "tempt" in the King James Version usually means "test." God tested Abraham to see whether he was willing to offer his son Isaac. The Lord permitted Satan to test Job. "And the Lord said to Satan, 'Behold, all that he has is in your power; only upon himself do not put forth your hand'" (Job 1:12). We read in Matthew 4:1, "Then Jesus was led up by the Spirit into the wilderness to be tempted by the devil." The Holy Spirit led Jesus to the battlefield, but the devil did the tempting.

The devil is the origin of all evil, including all temptation. We read in Luke 22:3, "Then Satan entered into Judas called Iscariot, who was of the number of the twelve." He led him to betray Jesus. Jesus said to Simon Peter: "Simon, Simon, behold, Satan demanded to have you, that he might sift you like wheat, but I have prayed for you that your faith may not fail" (Luke vv. 31, 32). The Bible does not explain the origin of Satan, but very early in the very first book Satan is shown enticing Eve to sin. Jesus said of Satan, "He was a murderer from the beginning, and has nothing to do with the truth, because there is no truth in him. When he lies, he speaks according to his own nature, for he is a liar and the father of lies" (John 8:44).

A person is tempted to do evil by the evil that dwells in his heart. "Each person is tempted when he is lured and enticed by his own desire. Then desire when it has conceived gives birth to sin; and sin when it is full-grown brings forth death" (James 1:14, 15). Our Lord declared: "For from within, out of the heart of man, come evil thoughts, fornication, theft, murder, adultery, coveting, wickedness, deceit, licentiousness, envy, slander, pride, foolishness. All these evil things come from within, and they defile a man" (Mark 7:21–23).

One may be tempted by his foes and by his friends. Our enemies may deliberately entice us into sin by offering us temptations. They may lay traps and seek to lure us by false promises. The world may lure us by its pleasures. Even our friends may tempt us, not deliberately or with evil motives, but by wrong example and bad counsel. Because of one's love for his family he may be tempted to steal to provide for the necessities or even the luxuries of life.

We are not only tempted at our weakest points but at our strongest. That was true of Samson. His weakest point was his trust in bad women, and they got him into many troubles. His strongest point was his vow to God, symbolized by his long hair, and this is where the enemy conquered Samson. Some people, who would never be tempted to get drunk, may be tempted into pride or hypocrisy or self-righteousness and judgment of others. This may be the preacher's temptation. Not many of us have ever been tempted to get drunk, but how many of us have been tempted to be proud!

We are tempted from without and from within, from the world and from our own sinful nature. All of us are sometimes tempted. Jesus himself was "one who in every respect has been tempted as we are, yet without sinning" (Heb. 4:15). The best and the worst, the wisest and the most foolish, the richest and the poorest, the learned and the ignorant—all are tempted. "Therefore let any one who thinks that he stands take heed lest he fall" (1 Cor. 10:12). Paul goes ahead to declare that our temptations are common to all men. "No temptation has overtaken you that is not common to man. God is faithful, and he will not let you be tempted beyond your strength, but with the temptation will also provide the way of escape, that you may be able to endure it" (v. 13).

Now what is our defense against temptation? How may we be delivered from the evil one? Jesus says we are to pray for divine guidance, that God will lead us in paths of righteousness and away from temptation. God has never led anyone into sin and will never do so. We are to pray that he will lead us away from it, into paths of truth and holiness. This is a positive prayer.

We are to look to Jesus for help. "Because he himself has suffered and been tempted, he is able to help those who are tempted" (Heb. 2:18). The devil tried every kind of temptation on Jesus, but Jesus withstood him. Jesus is therefore able to help us. We are to "run with perseverance the race that is set before us, looking to Jesus the pioneer and perfecter of our faith" (Heb. 12:1, 2).

We are to follow the guidance of the Holy Spirit. Jesus promised: "When the Spirit of truth comes, he will guide you into all the truth" (John 16:13). He will lead us through our enlightened Christian conscience.

Again, in the fight against temptation and the devil, we are to remember who we are and maintain our self-respect. When Joseph was tempted by Potiphar's wife he refused to yield, saying, "How then can I do this great wickedness, and sin against God?" (Gen. 39:9). Others might do it, but Joseph was a true servant of the Lord and could never stoop to such a sin. When Nehemiah was in peril of his life, he was tempted to flee into the temple for safety, but he said, "Should such a man as I flee? And what man such as I could go into the temple and live? I will not go in" (Neh. 6:11). He would not play the coward to save his own skin. We are children of God. To remember that fact will help to keep us true and faithful and strong.

We are to remember those who love and trust us and those whom we love and trust. Many a person has been kept from sin by remembering a dear parent, or a loving wife, or a devoted husband, or a trusting child. We are to remember all those who really care for us, and we are to refuse to hurt them by yielding to temptation and sin.

We also have the defense of the Bible. Jesus used the Scriptures against the devil. Each time the devil tempted him, Jesus quoted the Scriptures, "It is written" (Matt. 4:4, 7, 10). That settled it for Jesus. We are to know our Bible and use it in fighting against the devil. We are to lay up God's word in our hearts that we may avoid sin (Ps. 119:11).

Finally we are to put on the whole armor of God. Paul wrote:

> Put on the whole armor of God, that you may be able to stand against the wiles of the devil. . . . Therefore take the whole armor of God, that you may be able to withstand in the evil day, and having done all, to stand. Stand therefore, having girded your loins with truth, and having put on the breastplate of righteousness, and having shod your feet with the equipment of the gospel of peace; above all taking the shield of faith, with which you can quench all the flaming darts of the evil one. And take the helmet of salvation, and the sword of the Spirit, which is the word of God. (Eph 6:11, 13–17)

Notice that this armor includes truth, righteousness, the gospel, faith, salvation, the Spirit, and the word of God. If we fortify ourselves with this armor, we shall overcome the evil one. Jesus promised that no one would ever be able to snatch us, his sheep, out of his hand or out of his Father's hand.

We can begin a new year or a new day with confidence that God will guide us away from temptation into paths of righteousness, and that he will deliver us from Satan and sin if we look to him in faith, if we live as his children, and if we follow his divine leadership.

We should begin every new year with the prayer that Jesus taught us: "Our Father who art in heaven, Hallowed be thy name. Thy kingdom come, Thy will be done, On earth as it is in heaven. Give us this day our daily bread; And forgive us our debts, As we also have forgiven our debtors; And lead us not into temptation, But deliver us from evil" (Matt. 6:9–13). "For thine is the kingdom and the power and the glory, for ever. Amen" (Matt. 6:13, margin).

If we pray this prayer in the right spirit, we shall be ready for every new year and every new day, and shall march through it with courage and confidence, born of a true faith in the Father, the Son, and the Holy Spirit.

7

Learning How to Pray

"Lord, teach us to pray" (Luke 11:1).

One day the disciples of Jesus heard and saw him pray. They were impressed by his praying, and one of them said to him, "Lord, teach us to pray, as John taught his disciples." Doubtless these disciples had heard and seen Jesus pray on many occasions. His prayers were different and more real than any they had ever heard. His prayer made them feel that they did not really know how to pray. How many of us feel the same way? Most of us, who have been praying for many years, sometimes feel that we know very little about this wonderful power of prayer. We need to say to Jesus Christ, "Lord, teach us to pray."

In answer to this request, Jesus gave his disciples what we commonly call "The Lord's Prayer." It is really the model prayer, an outline to guide us as we pray. I do not believe that Jesus meant for us simply to repeat the words of it as a ritual. That may be proper to do occasionally, but simply to repeat it is not really to pray. However, if we look upon this as an outline to guide us in our praying, it will be very helpful. For it includes everything that we should ever pray for.

We have already looked in some detail at the various ideas and petitions in this prayer as recorded in Matthew 6:9–13, and here we shall repeat some of those things. However, we shall now examine the words of Jesus more closely, to grasp some great principles that we should recognize and follow in our praying. There are eight of these principles as set forth in this model prayer.

The first principle that should guide us is the fatherhood of God. When we pray we are to say, "Our Father who art in heaven." As Creator of the world God is Father of all. He created all men in his own spiritual image. Every man everywhere, regardless of race or nationality, is a child of God in this sense, and most men feel that there is some Being above them to whom they are responsible. But here Jesus was talking to his own disciples who through faith in him as God's Son had been given the special right to call God Father. They had received God's Son in faith, and God had adopted them into his family. They had experienced a spiritual birth through the Holy Spirit that made them a new creation in Christ.

True prayer is a fellowship between a child and his heavenly Father. It is real communion. There is a feeling of oneness and companionship. The child is confident of the Father's love and concern. He responds to the love of God and desires to feel the presence of God in his life. Jesus habitually addressed God as Father and taught his disciples to look upon God as their loving Father also, far better to them than any earthly father could ever be. Jesus was saying in substance: Think of the very best earthly father you know, consider his love and goodness to his own children; then multiply that over and over again, and you begin to get a true picture of God. As he said: "Or what man of you, if his son asks him for bread, will give him a stone? Or if he asks for a fish, will give him a serpent? If you then, who are evil, know how to give good gifts to your children, how much more will your Father who is in heaven give good things to those who ask him!" (Matt. 7:9–11). God is more loving, more gracious, more understanding, more generous, and far more able to give all that we need. So Jesus teaches us that true prayer is fellowship, or communion, between a loving heavenly Father and his child. The child seeks to please his Father and to express his love to him and enjoy his presence.

The second principle of prayer is the brotherhood of all believers. This is seen in the pronoun "our." We are to pray, saying, "Our Father"; he is not only my Father. Every Christian is a member of one large family of God, and in our praying we are to be guided by this truth. Understanding this will keep us from making any selfish prayers. We are to ask for nothing that would hurt our brothers or deprive them of their rights. Brotherly love is to be manifested in every area of life, and certainly in our prayer life.

We are to pray together, saying, "Our Father." That is what we do in church. The pastor does not do all the praying, he leads in prayer. Jesus said on another occasion, "Again I say to you, if two of you agree on earth about anything they ask, it will be done for them by my Father in heaven. For where two or three are gathered in my name, there am I in the midst of them" (Matt. 18:19, 20). Of course this does not mean that we are not to pray alone also. Probably most of our prayers will be said in private, in our own secret place alone with God. Even in that secret place we are to remember our Christian brothers and ask only for what would help them as well as ourselves.

The third principle is the principle of reverence or respect for God. "Hallowed be thy name" comes right after we call God Father. The meaning of "name" includes the very nature and character and person of God. This means that, while God is a loving Father, we are to recognize that he is God and not man. We must stand in holy awe, what the Bible calls the fear of God when we pray. We dare not be flippant, careless, irreverent, or disrespectful. Over familiarity with God is as repulsive as overfamiliarity with a king, and far more so. God is holy, unique in righteousness and majestic in glory and splendor.

With this principle in sight we will not ask God for anything that a holy God could not give without compromising his character. His gifts are always in keeping with his character as a holy and gracious and good God. We should ask only for what is right, worthy, and good. A righteous and holy God could never grant an unrighteous or unholy petition. God will grant only that which will bring glory to his holy name. Our prayers are to be in the name of Jesus, which means that they are to be in keeping with his character, in accord with his nature, for the good of his kingdom. We pray, saying, "For his name's sake," for his benefit, his welfare, the advancement of his kingdom and his cause. Jesus prayed according to this principle, as we shall observe when we study his great prayer in the seventeenth chapter of John and his other prayers.

The next principle we are to recognize is the absolute lordship of Jesus Christ when we pray, "Thy kingdom come." For God and Christ are one. God's kingdom is Christ's kingdom. God reigns through Christ. Jesus spoke of my kingdom and referred to himself as King. Others called him "King of kings and Lord of lords" (Rev. 19:16). So in all our praying we are to recognize the sovereignty of the Lord Jesus Christ and acknowledge his right to rule in our lives and in the hearts of those who claim him as Savior. We are to pray for the coming of his kingdom, for his enthronement as King in the hearts of all people everywhere. This petition involves a pledge to work for the King. We are his ambassadors and representatives in this world and are to "seek first his kingdom and his righteousness" (Matt. 6:33).

The fifth principle of right praying is the loving purpose or desire or will of God: "Thy will be done, On earth as it is in heaven." We are to seek for nothing contrary to his will, his desire, his purpose. We should never seek to change God's will, for his will is always right. Prayer Changes Things! That is a good motto, but it changes us, not the nature of God. Our wills are to conform to his holy will, to become one with his divine will. Prayer changes us and seeks to make our wills conform to the righteous will of our loving heavenly Father. Jesus recognized this in his own praying. In Gethsemane he prayed, "My Father, if it be possible, let this cup pass from me; nevertheless, not as I will, but as thou wilt. . . . My Father, if this cannot pass unless I drink it, thy will be done" (Matt. 26:39, 42). Jesus made the will of God his guiding principle in his praying and in his living.

God's will is to be done here and now: "On earth as it is in heaven." The Christian religion is something that has to do with every aspect of life on earth. It is not other worldly but this worldly. It affects all life here and now and forever. Consequently, the gospel of Jesus has social implications. It changes society by changing men and women and children. That is the only way society can actually be changed—by changing the character of people through the regenerating power of the Spirit of truth. We are to make the earth a colony of heaven. Jesus is one day to reign supremely in a new heaven and a new earth. The secret of a good life is conformity to the will of God. We can discover that will through prayer and Bible study. If we really desire to do his will, we will have little or no trouble discovering God's will.

A sixth principle of prayer is a spirit of dependence on God to supply our material and physical needs. Following the model prayer we ask God to "Give us this day our daily bread." As we have seen, bread represents all our physical and material needs. We are really praying: "Lord, give us what we need for our bodies: food, clothing, shelter, health." This is day-by-day dependence upon God. We live just a day at a time. We are not to hoard our bread. The manna in the wilderness was good for only a day at a time; only on the day before the sabbath could an extra amount be gathered for the sabbath day itself. On the other six days it had to be gathered fresh every morning. Jesus teaches us to recognize our constant dependence upon God. God will supply our bread as we trust him. He has filled the earth with a bountiful supply of food for every man and for every creature. If some are hungry while some are overfed, it is because some of us grab more than our share. We are to pray this prayer as brothers, saying, "Give *us* this day *our* daily bread." We are to share food and material things with our brothers everywhere.

The next principle to guide us is our dependence upon God to supply our spiritual needs as well as our physical needs. We are dependent upon him for forgiveness of our sins. Our sins are debts which we owe. We are hopelessly in debt to God, but his redeeming grace cancels the debt when we pray earnestly for his pardon and mercy. The entire New Testament emphasizes the wonderful truth that in Jesus Christ who died upon the cross every believer has forgiveness, cleaning, reconciliation, peace, salvation, and eternal life. Every spiritual need is supplied through Jesus Christ.

Then we are to pray for God's guidance and protection: "And lead us not into temptation, But deliver us from evil" (Matt. 6:13). We are to pray that God may lead us away from every evil temptation and protect us from the evil one who seeks to draw us away by our own lusts and entice us into sin. We are asking God to lead us always in his way of truth and holiness, to protect us from the power of evil or the evil one, who is Satan or the devil. We pray for deliverance from Satan, sin, and death.

Scholars tell us that the closing of the Lord's Prayer was probably added by Christians who used this model prayer in their public worship. They added the closing praise: "For thine is the kingdom and the power and the glory, for ever. Amen." We can use the same ascription when we use the model prayer as the guide for our praying. When we see in the Lord's Prayer an outline for our praying, we have learned the lesson of the early disciples when they said to Jesus, "Lord, teach us to pray."

8

God Answers Prayer

"If you then, who are evil, know how to give good gifts to your children, how much more will the heavenly Father give the Holy Spirit to those who ask him!" (Luke 11:13).

God answers prayer! Do we really believe that? Do we actually believe that God always hears and answers our prayers? I have heard some claim that God has not answered their prayers. At times we have all felt that our praying was in vain. We have prayed for things and have not received them. We may mistakenly think that God has not answered our prayers because we have not immediately received what we asked for. We may ask for fruit, and God answers by giving us a seed that must first be planted to grow into a tree and only after a few years will bear fruit. That takes a long time. The world asked for a savior, and God answered by sending a little baby to a manger, who would take years to grow and advance until his hour for saving the world had arrived thirty or more years later. So God sometimes answers by saying, "Wait."

We may conclude that God does not answer our prayers because we do not get exactly what we ask for. But would it be wise for God to give us always exactly what we ask for? We often ask for things that would be harmful to us and to others. We may ask for things that we really do not want, even though we think we do at the moment. God knows our hearts better than we do, and when we pray God answers. We sometimes may not recognize his answer, but we always get something better than we asked for.

According to Luke's Gospel, after teaching his disciples to pray, Jesus went on with a parable to show his disciples why men pray, how men pray, and why God answers prayer.

We pray because we are aware of some need, a need that we ourselves cannot supply. Something is lacking, and we pray because we believe that God can and will answer.

Jesus told of an embarrassed host who had an unexpected visitor at midnight. This hour for visiting was not too unusual, for in those days many traveled at night to avoid the heat of the day. No provision had been made by the host to entertain visitors, yet custom demanded that he provide food and shelter for his friend. There were few inns in that day, and according to biblical scholars, those that did exist were uncomfortable and dangerous places to stay. So travelers depended upon the hospitality of friends along the way—a custom in our own country just a few decades ago. But this host had very little food in the house, and the markets were closed for the night. There was no such thing as stores that stayed open twenty-four hours a day. So this man went knocking on his neighbor's door. "Friend, lend me three loaves; for a friend of mine has arrived on a journey, and I have nothing to set before him" (Luke 11:5, 6).

Despite the physical details, this is actually a picture of man's spiritual need. We all have needs which we cannot supply. No amount of work or striving can really meet our spiritual needs. We need salvation from sin more than anything else, but we are completely helpless to save ourselves. Reform, education, culture, wealth, fame—none of these can redeem us from sin. We need power to live victoriously. We do not possess this power in ourselves; it must come from God through Christ alone. A midnight of trouble may come to us. We may have an unexpected visitor in the form of sickness, suffering, pain, misery; or in the form of anxiety, worry, fear; or in the form of guilt and a sense of sinfulness.

We must first be conscious of our need. The self-satisfied soul never really prays. He may parade his virtues before the Lord like the proud Pharisee in the temple, but he does not really pray.

The embarrassed host in the parable had a neighbor to whom he could go, a person who was really his friend, although he was surly and gruff. He had a big heart in spite of his rough outside.

We know that we have a Friend, even the heavenly Father, who can supply our needs at midday or at midnight or at any time. He is never surly and gruff, but always kind and generous. Paul wrote of this Friend, saying, "And my God will supply every need of yours according to his riches in glory in Christ Jesus" (Phil. 4:19). God has an inexhaustible supply of riches in his heavenly storehouse. He is able, willing, and ready to supply every need of his children, who are more than friends—they are members of his own spiritual family and citizens of his kingdom.

This parable shows not only why men pray but also how men pray. The embarrassed host went directly to his friend. He did not send a servant, but went himself. And we are to go personally and directly to our heavenly Father, not through a priest or even a church. The poorest sinner can approach the throne of God boldly, confident that he will receive a hearing as he makes his requests.

The host in the parable was frank and specific. He stated the true facts and conditions; he told it like it was. He knew exactly what he needed: "Friend, lend me three loaves." We must tell God our true condition. We cannot hide anything from him. He knows our hearts, our thoughts, our desires, and our needs. We must be completely honest and sincere, and we should always be specific in our praying. Often our prayers are too general: "Bless us and help us, O Lord!" we pray. But we should be more definite. We should call the names of our friends before the throne of grace and tell our loving Father exactly what we feel and what we need.

This embarrassed host in the parable was shamelessly persistent. That is what "importunity" (Luke 11:8) means. He was "troublesomely urgent: overly persistent in request or demand." This man was not at all shy or timid. He kept banging on the door of his friend's house until he heard a response from within. When he made his request he heard a gruff answer, "Do not bother me; the door is now shut, and my children are with me in bed; I cannot get up and give you anything" (v. 7). We can all sympathize with him, especially if we have had small children in the house and have just gotten them to sleep and have just fallen asleep ourselves when the doorbell rings. No one really likes to be awakened at a time like that. But this importunate host kept on rapping on the door and asking for food until he got it.

He was like the Canaanite woman whose little daughter needed help. She was stubbornly persistent until she got what she wanted and needed. (Matt. 15:21–28). Blind Bartimaeus also kept begging until he got his sight restored (Mark 10:46–52).

Why should we be so persistent in our praying? Is God reluctant to grant our requests? Is he too busy to be bothered? Does he answer us gruffly and rudely? No, Jesus is showing a contrast, not a likeness. He is saying in effect: If a grumpy friend would give in to persistent pleading, how much more would a loving Father in heaven answer the prayers of his dear children! We need to be persistent as an evidence of our own earnest desires. A parent cannot give a child an education until the child wants it. God cannot give us many things until we earnestly and eagerly want them. We may have to agonize for them, like Jacob who wrestled with the angel of the Lord until he received his blessing. What are we really praying for today? Maybe not for the things that our lips ask for, but for the things that our hearts crave.

This parable of Jesus shows not only why and how men pray, but it shows also why God answers prayer. Jesus interpreted his parable by saying: "I tell you, though he will not get up and give him anything because he is his friend, yet because of his importunity he will rise and give him whatever he needs. And I tell you, Ask, and it will be given you; seek, and you will find; knock, and it will be opened to you. For every one who asks receives, and he who seeks finds, and to him who knocks it will be opened" (Luke 11:8–10). The tenses of the verbs here mean continued action: keep on asking, keep on seeking, keep on knocking. First we ask in words; then we ask in effort to find the right answer; and then we work until we get what we want. Our God expects us to help answer our prayers for ourselves. In fact, he does not do for us what we can do for ourselves. The lazy man may blame God for not answering his prayers, when the whole trouble lies in his own sloth.

Then Jesus went further in the interpretation of this parable. "What father among you, if his son asks for a fish, will instead of a fish give him a serpent; or if he asks for an egg, will give him a scorpion?" (vv. 11, 12). No earthly father who deserves the name would deceive his children by substituting a serpent for a fish or a scorpion for an egg. If no earthly father would so deceive his children, how unthinkable to believe that a loving heavenly Father would do so! God does not give us some poor substitute that would hurt us. He does not give us less than we ask for, but more.

Jesus applies this parable by saying: "If you then, who are evil, know how to give good gifts to your children, how much more will the heavenly Father give the Holy Spirit to those who ask him!" (v. 13). It is natural for any normal parent to love his children and give them what they need if he can. God is not evil but eternally good. He is merciful, kind, loving, and wise. He is also rich in treasures and able to give all things. Therefore he gives always the very best to his children. The best gift is his Holy Spirit, for that gift includes all else: Father, Son, and Holy Spirit: Three in One. That gift means salvation, eternal life, wisdom, truth, joy, power, and victory.

Here Jesus is saying that the very nature and character of God assures answered prayer. God is loving, and his gifts are the expressions of divine love. God is good, and his gifts are intended for our highest welfare. God is wise, and his gifts are always in our best interests. God is righteous, and his gifts are always right. He is just, and his gifts are always fair. He is generous, and his gifts are always abundant.

Such a God always answers prayer. Sometimes he says, "No!" because that is the best answer. Sometimes he says, "Wait!" for it may take months or even years before we are really ready to receive what he wants to give us. Sometimes he says, "Yes!" and the answer may come before we rise from our knees. Someone very wisely and truly said, "He who rises from his knees a better man has already received the answer to his prayers."

9

Life as a Prayer

"And he told them a parable, to the effect that they ought always to pray and not lose heart" (Luke 18:1).

How much do we pray? Some who do not spend much time on their knees at prayer may do more actual praying than others who spend hours in what they consider praying. We are frequently told that we ought to pray more, and that is surely good advice, for too many of us are ineffective in our praying. We may think we are praying when in reality we are not. On the other hand, we may think that we never pray, when actually we are praying more than we realize. Does this make any sense? Can we live our life as a prayer?

Luke wrote: "And he told them a parable, to the effect that they ought always to pray and not lose heart" (Luke 18:1). Does this mean that we ought to spend all our time saying prayers? Some people live apart in monasteries or convents in order spend many hours saying prayers. Others spend hours upon their knees.

This pattern may give the impression that its followers are very religious, and they may in truth be so. But Jesus did not spend all his time upon his knees or saying prayers. He did not neglect to pray; but he was busy healing the sick, preaching the gospel of the kingdom, teaching spiritual truth, feeding the hungry, comforting the sorrowful, and ministering to the needy. Yet there was no conflict between his praying and his working. They were often one and the same.

What is prayer anyway? Is it more than saying prayers? We ought to say our prayers, and Jesus did that. But true prayer is a life attitude. It is living constantly in the presence of God, having fellowship with the divine, being aware of God's presence all the time. James Montgomery expressed this idea in a meaningful and beautiful hymn.

> Prayer is the soul's sincere desire,
> Uttered or unexpressed;
> The motion of a hidden fire
> That trembles in the breast.

Words and forms are not always necessary when we pray. Words are often too feeble to express the deepest feelings of the heart, and sometimes they even interfere with true fellowship. As we have noted, the Lord's Prayer is more an outline of prayer, a guideline to help us organize our thoughts, than it is something to repeat frequently without feeling or without sensing the deep meaning of the words or expressing the true longing of our hearts.

When Jesus said that we should always pray, he meant that true prayer is an attitude and an atmosphere that covers the whole of life. We ought never to get into any mood or mental or spiritual attitude where praying would be out of place. Two preachers at an association meeting once got into a heated argument. One finally turned to the other and said, "Brother ______ please lead us in prayer." "Pray yourself: I'm in no mood to pray!" came the response.

Many people pray only when they are conscious of a deep need. Perhaps physical sickness or suffering has driven them to prayer. We all need to pray at such times, and most of us surely do. James wrote, "Is any one among you suffering? Let him pray" (James 5:13). It is often easy to get people to pray at such times. I heard of a preacher visiting a hospital, who asked the patient if he wanted to be prayed for. "Oh, no," he replied, "I'm not that sick!" When we are in physical danger on a battlefield or during a violent storm or in some other peril, we find it natural to pray. When heavy burdens must be borne, when sorrows and bereavements and troubles come, it is easy to pray. Read the psalms and observe how often the psalmist was praying during perilous days. It is natural to pray when death comes to a loved one or when we ourselves face death. Most of us pray during the crises of life.

But we should also pray when things seem to be well. During times of prosperity we may need to pray even more than during times of adversity. Prayer should permeate all our life. Prayer is an attitude and an atmosphere that should surround us and cover us like a spiritual blanket. "An attitude of gratitude," that is a real prayer. We should live in an attitude of love, kindness, gentleness, and goodness. So Jesus is teaching us here that we should always live in such an attitude to have unbroken fellowship with God. That is prayer at its best.

Jesus went on to say that we should "pray and not lose heart" (some versions say, "and not faint"). Some people only pray when they are fainting or about to lose heart through discouragement. But Jesus is saying that constant, true prayer will keep us from losing heart, from fainting. People faint and lose heart because they do not pray. They are often weak, helpless, and weary because they rely upon their own strength and try to do things without the help of God. That was true even of the inner circle of Christ's disciples in Gethsemane. They fell asleep while Jesus prayed in agony. They did not "watch and pray" as he had asked them (Matt. 26:38–45). On another occasion, other disciples could not cure the epileptic boy at the foot of the Mount of Transfiguration because they failed to pray (Mark 9:17, 18). Many of life's failures are due to prayerlessness, to an attitude of mistrust, rebellion, or hostility toward God. The wrong attitude brings failure.

Life apart from God means failure. Defeat is inevitable to the nonpraying person. The atheist has the laws of God against him: "From heaven fought the stars, from their courses they fought against Sisera" (Judg. 5:20). In other words, the atheist, the nonpraying person, has the whole universe arrayed against him. In one of the greatest passages of the Bible we read: "He gives power to the faint, and to him who has no might he increases strength. Even youths shall faint and be weary, and young men shall fall exhausted; but they who wait for the Lord shall renew their strength, they shall mount up with wings like eagles, they shall run and not be weary, they shall walk and not faint" (Isa. 40:29–31).

Thus it is that true prayer keeps one from fainting,

for he lives in the atmosphere of God, who gives him power and victory. Such a person can say with Robert Browning's "Paracelsus":

> If I stoop
> Into a dark tremendous sea of cloud,
> It is but for a time;
> I press God's lamp
> Close to my breast;
> Its splendor soon or late,
> Will pierce the gloom:
> I shall emerge one day

The world may crucify the praying man, but his cross will spell victory. Trials and burdens may come, but God delivers him from them all. Isaiah wrote centuries ago a truth that is unchanging: "Thou dost keep him in perfect peace, whose mind is stayed on thee, because he trusts in thee" (Isa. 26:3). The praying man is the one whose mind is permanently stayed or fixed on God. God is always near and ready to help such a man and to keep him from losing heart.

Jesus went on to tell another parable to illustrate this truth. He told of a widow who was seeking legal justice. Widows had a hard time in that day. Perhaps some Pharisee had been devouring her house. "Woe to you, scribes and Pharisees, hypocrites!" said Jesus on another occasion, "for you devour widow's houses and for a pretense you make long prayers" (Matt. 23:14). The widow in this parable kept coming again and again to a certain judge, saying, "Vindicate me against my adversary" (Luke 18:3). Now this judge, was one "who neither feared God nor regarded man" (v. 2). For a while the judge refused to give this widow justice. But when she kept coming and persisting in her plea, the judge finally said, "Though I neither fear God nor regard man, yet because this widow bothers me, I will vindicate her, or she will wear me out by her continual coming" (vv. 4, 5). There were several ways of dealing with such judges. They could be bribed, but that was probably beyond the ability of a poor widow. They could be intimidated by threatening to report them to some superior authority; or they could be nagged until they finally relented to get rid of their worrisome petitioners. This widow kept coming back and probably used every weapon at her disposal, until the judge finally gave in because of her dogged persistence and stubbornness.

Jesus applied the truth of this parable by saying, "And will not God vindicate his elect, who cry to him day and night? Will he delay long over them? I tell you, he will vindicate them speedily" (vv. 7, 8). Observe carefully the argument of Jesus here. He is saying in effect: If a hard-hearted and wicked judge will finally give justice to a persistent widow just to get her off his back and save himself from possible violence and threats, how much more will a loving heavenly Father who is good and kind and merciful, give justice to his chosen ones who live always in the attitude of prayer! Jesus is showing the great contrast between a loving God and a wicked judge. God is always ready to answer the prayers of his children who come to him day and night. We are to be persistent with God, not because he is reluctant to grant the requests of his children—we do not need to persuade God—but because we need to make certain in our own minds what our real desires and needs are. We sometimes ask God for things we do not truly want and for things we certainly do not need. Sometimes our petitions are foolish. When we live in constant fellowship and communion with our living heavenly Father, we learn more and more what we really need and what is best for us. God always grants the best.

Is our life a life of prayer? Are we conscious of the living presence of God? We do not have to be on our knees. God may say to us as he said to Moses: "Why do you cry to me? Tell the people of Israel to go forward" (Exod. 14:15). God may say, "Get up from your knees and roll up your sleeves and help me answer your prayers." For we do help God answer our prayers by living constantly in his divine presence and being ready always to pray and not lose heart.

If we live constantly in the attitude and spirit of prayer, we shall indeed never lose heart or be faint. Such an attitude will keep us from being like the pagans who "heap up empty phrases" and "think that they will be heard for their many words" (Matt. 6:7).

10

Two Sinners Praying

"Two men went up into the temple to pray, one a Pharisee and the other a tax collector" (Luke 18:10).

This parable about the two men praying in the temple follows immediately the parable we have just considered about life as a prayer. Luke tells us that Jesus spoke this parable "to some who trusted in themselves that they were righteous and despised others" (Luke 18:9). Jesus observed men as they prayed. He noticed their attitudes, their words, and their motives. Today he hears all who pray and knows what lies behind it and what is involved in it.

Jesus knew about the Pharisees and the tax collectors. Here he looks at two men praying. Let us look with Jesus and try to see what he observed and consider his comments.

First, look at the Pharisee: Jesus said, "The Pharisee stood and prayed thus with himself" (v. 11). Nothing was wrong with his physical attitude. Some people think that one cannot truly pray except on his knees. But many people on their knees think more of their physical discomfort than of what they are saying. They could pray with better concentration in a more comfortable position. Do not think that getting down on your knees makes you any more pious than standing on your feet. Choose the position that is best for you; so long as you are reverent and able to keep your mind on God, the physical position of the body is not important. The trouble with this Pharisee was that he "prayed thus with himself." He was not praying to God. Jesus had said in his Sermon on the Mount, "Beware of practicing your piety before men in order to be seen by them; for then you will have no reward from your Father who is in heaven" (Matt. 6:1).

Now this Pharisee had some good qualities. He was a man of prayer who went to the temple to pray for it was "the house of prayer." Some Pharisees were said to have prayed eighteen times a day. Most of them prayed at least three times a day: at nine o'clock in the morning, at twelve o'clock noon, and at three o'clock in the afternoon.

Before we condemn this Pharisee, let us examine our own prayer life. How many of us pray as often as he? Jesus said that men "ought always to pray," and yet some of us never pray at all. The Bible emphasizes prayer, and its great saints were devout persons of prayer. We are not to be like "the hypocrites; for they love to stand and pray in the synagogues and at the street corners, that they may be seen by men" (v. 5). Jesus warns us also not to "heap up empty phrases as the Gentiles do; for they think that they will be heard for their many words" (v. 7). Jesus said, "Your Father knows what you need before you ask him" (v. 8). But we are not to neglect our prayer life if we would be victorious Christians.

The Pharisee went on to say, "I fast twice a week" (Luke 18:12). The Mosaic law required fasting only on the Day of Atonement, but the Pharisees fasted often and thought that by fasting twice a week they were being super pious.

Many of us would be better off physically, and perhaps spiritually as well, if we fasted more. We are apt to feast more than we fast. The only difference between feasting and fasting is one little letter, but that literally makes a whale of a difference. Now Jesus did not emphasize fasting. Many people of his day did not have enough to eat anyway. The Pharisees had once asked him, "Why do you eat and drink with tax collectors and sinners? . . . The disciples of John fast often and offer prayers, and so do the disciples of the Pharisees, but yours eat and drink" (Luke 5:30, 33). Jesus replied, "Can you make wedding guests fast while the bridegroom is with them? The days will come, when the bridegroom is taken away from them, and then they will fast in those days" (vv. 34, 35).

Do we today practice our religious duties as faithfully as this Pharisee practiced his?

This Pharisee in the parable read his Bible. All Pharisees did that. They knew the letter of the law, although many of them had missed its true spirit and misread its meaning. Today many of us may be quite ignorant of our Bibles. We do not know its letter or its spirit. We cannot condemn this man unless we are as faithful in Bible study as was he.

Then he was a member of his church and was seeking to be faithful. It was not the church of Jesus Christ; that had not yet been formed, but he considered himself a follower of God and frequently went to God's house. He, like all Pharisees, was very strict in seeking to observe God's laws and all that he thought God had commanded.

Today the pastor's heart is often crushed and the hearts of God's faithful people broken when so many of the church members never attend or come so irregularly and do so little that their spiritual life is not even lukewarm; it is as cold as ice.

Jesus said of the Pharisees: "Woe to you, scribes and Pharisees, hypocrites! for you traverse sea and land to make a single proselyte, and when he becomes a proselyte, you make him twice as much a child of hell as yourselves" (Matt. 23:15). Even this criticism shows that the Pharisee at least had some zeal in doing what he thought was right. How many church members have lost every spark of zeal and enthusiasm? That may be one reason why many people are not attracted to the church today.

This Pharisee was morally pure. He could not be classed with adulterers (Luke 18:11). He had been faithful to his marriage vows. He had not wrecked his home by shameful living. He was morally clean. That is saying a lot when we consider the day in which he lived. It was a day of lax morals, when men could divorce their wives at will. Jesus spoke of one woman who had had five husbands and was then living with a sixth man who was not her husband. How many today can match this Pharisee in his moral purity? Let him who is innocent cast the first stone.

Moreover, he was just in his business dealings. He could say that he did not belong to the group called "extortioners, unjust." He had not cheated or robbed the poor. He had not oppressed the widows and orphans. He had been fair and honest in all his business transactions. We commend him for these virtues.

They are certainly important and essential virtues in today's world. Are we as honest and just as he? Or do we belong to those who think that old-fashioned honesty belongs only to the squares and is on the other side of the generation gap?

This Pharisee was a very liberal giver. He could truthfully say, "I give tithes of all that I get" (v. 12). He went beyond the law in tithing. How wonderful! What a good church member he would make! Yet Jesus said on another occasion: "Woe to you, scribes and Pharisees, hypocrites! for you tithe mint and dill and cummin, and have neglected the weightier matters of the law, justice and mercy and faith; these you ought to have done, without neglecting the others" (Matt. 23:23).

Here is a Pharisee with many virtues. What preacher or church leader would not brag about getting such a person to join his church!

Let us turn now and look briefly at the tax collector. He had sold out to the enemy: Rome, for he had bargained with the power that had conquered his nation to collect the taxes for this foreign power. Tax collectors in that day were known for their extortion and unjust dealings. He had probably robbed widows and orphans and his fellowmen under the guise of doing only what the government required. In the popular mind the words "publican" and "sinner" were synonymous. They went together like pork and beans or horse and carriage. This man's selfishness and greed had made him a traitor to his own nation. Such men were excommunicated from the synagogue and were ostracized by their own people. He had been shunned and ignored, was never invited to weddings or parties, and was hated by all and considered a sinner and a traitor. He loved Caesar's gold more than Judah's God. He admitted—and correctly—that he was "a sinner" (Luke 18:13).

So Jesus pictures two men who went to church to pray. Some churches would give the Pharisee a front seat, even a seat up on the platform with the preacher; and they would give the tax collector a back seat or no seat at all.

Now observe the attitudes and words of these two men as they pray. Look at the Pharisee. He was arrogantly self-righteous. He was one of those to whom Jesus told this parable "who trusted in themselves that they were righteous and despised others" (v. 9). As we noted before, "The Pharisee stood and prayed thus with himself," not with God. He was one who desired to be seen of men. He felt no need of God. He already had it made and had risen by his own self-righteousness and super piety. He paraded his self-acquired virtues before the people and thought that God must surely be proud of him. We see his egotism in his opening words: "God, I thank thee that I am not like other men" (v. 11). He was superior to the crowd, in a class all to himself. He was critical of others. He looked down his nose at them, despising them and looking with contempt upon them. Others were "extortioners, unjust, adulterers" (v. 11). They were crooks, liars, and unrighteous. When he saw the tax collector he probably said to himself, they should throw that crook out of the temple; he is a disgrace to this holy place.

This Pharisee made a very human mistake. He compared himself with his fellowman and said, "I am better than he is." We need to compare ourselves with the Lord Jesus Christ to see how far we fall short in every way. But this man was oblivious of God and "prayed thus with himself." When we see God, as young Isaiah saw him in the temple centuries ago, we cry out, "Woe is me! For I am lost; for I am a man of unclean lips, and I dwell in the midst of a people of unclean lips; for my eyes have seen the King, the LORD of hosts!" (Isa 6:5). This Pharisee lacked humility, the virtue without which no man can see the kingdom of God, let alone enter it. He was not praying to God but boasting to the congregation.

Now observe the attitude of the tax collector. His was, in contrast, an attitude of deep humility. He was "standing far off" (Luke 18:13). He was ashamed even to "lift up his eyes to heaven," or to look God in the face. He had the only attitude acceptable for worship—humility.

He also had an attitude of repentance, for he "beat his breast," being grieved because of his sins. He had come, not to brag, but to repent. It was an attitude of confession. Hear him as he pleads with all his heart, "God, be merciful to me a sinner!" He was pleading for mercy, not justice. He was standing in the need of God's grace, his unmerited favor.

This is the attitude we all need as we pray. We must be humble to be heard. We must repent to be forgiven. We must confess to obtain mercy.

Now look at the significant comment of our blessed Lord. Speaking of the tax collector Jesus said, "I tell you, this man went down to his house justified rather than the other; for every one who exalts himself will be humbled, but he who humbles himself will be exalted" (v. 14).

Jesus condemned the proud Pharisee. He was a blind sinner who refused to acknowledge his sin. He was trusting in his own righteousness to get him by, like Saul of Tarsus before he found Christ as Savior. He was a lost sinner like the brother of the prodigal son.

He was like other Pharisees who could not see the virtues of the very Son of God because they were blinded by their own self-made halos.

Jesus commended the tax collector. He did not commend his sins of extortion and injustice. Jesus commended him for his spirit of humility, his act of repentance, and his confession and prayer for mercy. Jesus said that this tax collector went home "justified." That means God had forgiven, cleansed, and redeemed him and had accepted him as his child who had entered the kingdom in the right way. He was, as Paul later taught, justified by faith. Paul would have said to this tax collector: "But you were washed, you were sanctified, you were justified in the name of the Lord Jesus Christ and in the Spirit of our God" (1 Cor. 6:11).

Here is one of the easiest of Christ's parables to understand. May we come to God through Christ in a spirit of true humility, confessing our sins, repenting of them, and pleading for mercy. If we do that sincerely we can go home justified, and one day arrive at our eternal home and be accepted by a loving Father.

11

Watching and Praying

"Watch and pray that you may not enter into temptation" (Matt. 26:41).

Spiritual alertness and prayer are essential to successful Christian living. The Bible often warns against being spiritually asleep, inattentive, indifferent. It calls upon us to be spiritually alert, morally awake; and in order to be so we are told to watch and pray. Jesus used this expression several times: "Watch and pray!" It is alert praying that will help us follow the Lord and do his will, for the right kind of praying will keep us awake. These words of our Lord apply to all of life; we are to watch and pray.

What are we to watch?

Ourselves, first. "Take heed, watch," said Jesus in Mark 13:33. Again, he said, "Take heed to yourselves" (v. 9). We are often warned today: "Watch Your Step!" or "Watch Out!" What are we to watch about ourselves? We must guard against wrong thoughts, unclean, impure, lustful thoughts. We must avoid the attitudes of envy, jealousy, mistrust, hatred, suspicion, arrogance, pessimism, depression, and despair. The right kind of praying will help us cultivate the right kind of thoughts and attitudes. When we have an attitude of adoration, admiration, loyalty, and commitment in our relationship to Christ, our thoughts mold our character and govern our action. Bernard of Clairvaux centuries ago declared that the very thought of Jesus filled his breast with sweetness. Prayer will help us watch our attitudes.

Prayer will also help us watch our words. We must think twice before we speak—not speak twice before we think. We should say only what is kind, truthful, helpful, and fitting; not what is critical, harsh, unjust, and rude. Prayer will help us guard our lips. The Lord's brother James warned against the uncontrolled tongue:

> For we all make many mistakes, and if any one makes no mistakes in what he says he is a perfect man, able to bridle his whole body also. If we put bits into the mouths of horses that they may obey us, we guide their whole bodies. Look at the ships also; though they are so great and are driven by strong winds, they are guided by a very small rudder wherever the will of the pilot directs. So the tongue is a little member and boasts of great things. How great a forest is set ablaze by a small fire! (James 3:2–5)

James goes on to describe the tongue as a fire that no man can tame without divine help. It is "a restless evil, full of deadly poison. With it we bless the Lord and Father, and with it we curse men, who are made in the likeness of God. . . . My brethren, this ought not to be so" (vv. 8–10). Our Lord Jesus said: "I tell you, on the day of judgment men will render account for every careless word they utter; for by your words you will be justified, and by your words you will be condemned" (Matt. 12:36, 37). We are to watch and pray in order to speak the right words and use our tongues to bless and praise God and not to curse men.

We are to watch our deeds also. If our thoughts and words are right, our deeds will be right. So the right kind of praying will help us to take heed to ourselves and guard our thoughts, attitudes, words, and deeds.

The right kind of praying will also help us to watch other people in the right way. Jesus warned against false prophets, saying, "For false Christs and false prophets will arise and show great signs and wonders, so as to lead astray, if possible, even the elect" (Matt. 24:24). We must be on our guard against such prophets. Some are false because their information is false. They are ignorant of the truth, having misread and misunderstood the Holy Scriptures. Their intentions may be good, but they are false leaders. Some are false because they are evil. They are false in character and are, according to Jesus, "false prophets, who come to you in sheep's clothing but inwardly are ravenous wolves" (Matt. 7:15). They may do spectacular things, but they are hypocrites. We must stay mentally and morally awake when we read or hear the words of these false prophets. We must not swallow the half-baked ideas of religious fanatics, but are to read the Bible carefully, prayerfully, alertly, and intelligently.

We are also to watch for good prophets. There are good Christians, who are teaching and preaching the word of God in truth and love. They are looking for and earnestly waiting for the appearance of our Lord.

We are to be on watch also for opportunities to do

good. We are not to fold our arms in idleness to await the Lord's return, like some in Thessalonica did. The Lord has given his servants charge over his work and has commanded "the doorkeeper to be on the watch" (Mark 13:34). We must keep busy about the Lord's work and keep preaching the gospel to all nations before his return (v. 10). Watchful prayer will help us to do this.

We are to expect persecution, for Jesus said to his disciples:

> But take heed to yourselves; for they will deliver you up to councils; and you will be beaten in synagogues; and you will stand before governors and kings for my sake, to bear testimony before them. . . . And when they bring you to trial and deliver you up, do not be anxious beforehand what you are to say; but say whatever is given you in that hour, for it is not you who speak, but the Holy Spirit. . . . But he who endures to the end will be saved. (vv. 9, 11, 13)

Only the right kind of praying will prepare us for victory over persecution.

Then we are to watch world events. The disciples had remarked to the Lord about the magnificent buildings of the temple, but Jesus told them that one day the temple would be destroyed. When they asked him when this would take place, he answered,

> Take heed that no one leads you astray. . . . And when you hear of wars and rumors of wars, do not be alarmed; this must take place, but the end is not yet. For nation will rise against nation, and kingdom against kingdom; there will be earthquakes in various places, there will be famines; this is but the beginning of the sufferings. (vv. 5, 7, 8)

The destruction of Jerusalem would be only a symbol of his Second Coming. Today we are to see and to interpret world events in the light of New Testament teachings, and thus see God's purpose in history. We are to have faith in his love and wisdom, knowing assuredly that he will gain the victory and that the Christian will share in that victory.

We are to watch for the coming again of the Lord Jesus. One day if we are still alive we "will see the Son of man coming in clouds with great power and glory" (v. 26). Jesus goes on to say,

> But of that day or that hour no one knows, not even the angels in heaven, nor the Son, but only the Father. Take heed, watch; . . . for you do not know when the master of the house will come, in the evening, or at midnight, or at cockcrow, or in the morning—lest he come suddenly and find you asleep. And what I say to you I say to all: Watch. (vv. 32, 33, 35–37)

The most significant words of Jesus concerning his Second Coming are "Watch and pray!" Only watchful and alert praying will keep us ready for his return.

Why are we to watch and pray? Lest we enter into temptation. In Gethsemane Jesus said to his disciples, "Sit here, while I go yonder and pray" (Matt. 26:36). He took Peter, James, and John with him a little farther into the garden and said to them, "My soul is very sorrowful, even to death; remain here, and watch with me" (v. 38). He prayed as he faced his cross, but the disciples fell asleep. When he found them sleeping, he said to Peter, "So, could you not watch with me one hour? Watch and pray that you may not enter into temptation; the spirit indeed is willing, but the flesh is weak"

(vv. 40, 41). He went to pray again, and again they fell asleep. They failed him in his hour of crisis, because they did not watch and pray. He said to them, "Are you still sleeping and taking your rest? Behold, the hour is at hand, and the Son of man is betrayed into the hands of sinners" (v. 45).

An alert attitude of prayer will help us resist and overcome temptation. The devil is subtle and cunning and will take advantage of us if he catches us off guard, if he finds us in the wrong place or with the wrong crowd. Prayer opens the windows of heaven for us and lets the divine power of God come to our aid. Prayer will keep us from doubt, despair, and pessimism. It will keep us on the watch, alert and wide awake. Jesus recognized the weakness of the flesh, but prayer will help us overcome that weakness.

Jesus often warned that if we fail to watch, we may be surprised by the unexpected. He warned his disciples to be ever alert and watch and pray lest he return and find them unprepared to receive him. "Watch therefore, for you do not know on what day your Lord is coming. Therefore you also must be ready; for the Son of man is coming at an hour you do not expect" (Matt. 24:42, 44). To be prepared *now* is to be ready *then*. This is the chief teaching of Jesus about the time of his Second Coming: We are to "watch and pray!"

It is interesting to note that Jesus places watching and praying together. Unless we pray, our watching will be in the wrong direction, and we may be watching for the wrong things. The upward look of prayer will keep our eyes in the right direction and our hearts in the right place.

Unless we pray, our watching will be half-hearted and unfaithful. Prayer will keep us from going to sleep when we should stay awake, and from growing careless when we should be alert. Praying will help us interpret correctly what we see. We shall be able to discern the signs of the times, and God will show us the meaning of history.

Prayer helps us prepare for the glad day when our Lord will return or for our own going home to be with the Lord forever. It will keep us centered on God's will and purpose, and from being so absorbed in material things that we cannot see the spiritual.

The New Testament plainly teaches that Jesus is coming to earth again. He may come today, tomorrow, or a thousand years from now. But we shall all be brought into his presence whenever he comes or when we die, and that may be at any moment. It cannot be far away for many. So Jesus says to every one of us through his Holy Spirit: "Take heed, watch; for you do not know when the time will come" (Mark 13:33).

12

Conditions of Effective Prayer

"And when you pray . . ." (Matt. 6:5).

Jesus assumed that his disciples would pray. In fact, they had asked him to teach them how to pray. We have already studied some of things he taught them about prayer. We shall now try to gather together some of his scattered teachings on prayer to learn some of the conditions of effective praying.

The right spirit or attitude of the person is one essential condition of effective praying. Jesus stresses the importance of this, not only in praying, but in living. What is the right spirit to have as we pray?

To begin with, it must be the spirit of reverence. We have already noted in the model prayer that we are praying to a holy God, saying, "Hallowed be thy name" (Matt. 6:9). No Christian will pray in a flippant manner or in unbecoming language. Sometimes people are too familiar with God. He is our great Friend, it is true, but we must remember that he is not man but God.

We must remember that God said: "For my thoughts are not your thoughts, neither are your ways my ways, . . . For as the heavens are higher than the earth, so are my ways higher than your ways and my thoughts than your thoughts" (Isa. 55:8, 9). So when we approach the throne of God we are, like Moses, to take off our shoes because we are on holy ground.

Then we must have the spirit of humility. Jesus stressed this point in his parable of the Pharisee and the tax collector praying in the temple as we have seen. Throughout his teachings our Lord emphasized this attitude, and on more than one occasion he said, "For every one who exalts himself will be humbled, and he who humbles himself will be exalted" (Luke 14:11; 18:14). Pride is one of the chief sins of the people which keeps them from praying effectively.

Again, there must be a spirit of sincerity. Jesus hated hypocrisy and denounced it very strongly: "And when you pray, you must not be like the hypocrites; for they love to stand and pray in the synagogues and at the street corners, that they may be seen by men" (Matt. 6:5). They have already received the only reward they will ever get, for God will not honor such false praying. We must be utterly sincere, honest, and truthful in all our praying. Our Father already knows what we need and what we truly want. We cannot deceive him, and it is a sin even to try to do so.

Above all, we must have a forgiving spirit whenever we pray. Jesus said, "And whenever you stand praying, forgive, if you have anything against any one; so that your Father also who is in heaven may forgive you your trespasses" (Mark 11:25). Jesus taught us to pray for our own forgiveness, and then he said, "For if you forgive men their trespasses, your heavenly Father also will forgive you; but if you do not forgive men their trespasses, neither will your Father forgive your trespasses" (Matt. 6:14, 15). We noticed in a previous chapter the parable of the unmerciful servant (Matt. 18:23–35), in which Jesus says in effect that God will forgive us only to the extent and in the degree that we ourselves forgive others. We cannot receive divine forgiveness until we ourselves have the forgiving spirit.

It is also important to have the spirit of gratitude. This is often the very heart of prayer. The grateful person will have a constant desire in his heart to express his thankfulness to the God who has done and is doing so much for him. To be grateful for God's past blessings is often the very thing that opens our hearts to receive more of his blessings in the present. Like any parent, the heavenly Father also delights to give to the grateful child. Jesus was disappointed when only one of ten lepers whom he healed returned to thank him (Luke 17:18, 19).

The right spirit of prayer is the spirit of unselfishness. The prodigal son left home saying, "Give me," but he returned home saying, "Make me a servant." Of course, we will ask for things we want and need, but we should never pray selfishly. We should not ask for anything for ourselves if the reception of it would be harmful to others.

Our prayer should always have the spirit of penitence and a sense of deep need. Even the Christian saint needs to pray for pardon every day. We must confess our sins to God and ask for his grace. The more worthy we are, the more unworthy we seem to ourselves. We must remember that we are sinners saved by grace and that we are what we are only by God's unmerited favor and not by our merit or good works.

In addition to having the right spirit when we pray, our prayers should be in the name of Jesus Christ. Let us look at some words of our Lord on this matter. In the space of four chapters in John's Gospel Jesus speaks six times about praying in his name. He said: "Whatever you ask in my name, I will do it, that the Father may be glorified in the Son, if you ask anything in my name, I will do it." (John 14:13, 14). At first that seems to be an unconditional promise that we can ask anything under the sun and be assured of getting exactly what we ask for. But the condition is that what we ask must be in the name of Jesus Christ, and that is not a magic formula that we attach to our prayers. It means that what we ask is to be in the best interest of Christ and his kingdom. A business man employed by a firm may be given the privilege of doing business in the name of the firm. The treasurer of an organization or business may be empowered and authorized to sign checks in the name of the group or company which he represents. In the same way, we pray in the name of Jesus, or as his representative as we do business for him, the head of the body, his church. This will eliminate all selfish praying, because our prayers will be for his sake, in his name, for the best interest of his kingdom in the world. In John 15:16 we read, "You did not choose me, but I chose you and appointed you that you should go and bear fruit and that your fruit should abide; so that whatever you ask the Father in my name, he may give it to you." We have significant words of our Lord in John 16:23, 24: "In that day you will ask nothing of me. Truly, truly, I say to you, if you ask anything of the Father, he will give it to you in my name. Hitherto you have asked nothing in my name; ask, and you will receive, that your joy may be full." Jesus had been speaking of going away from them for a little while. He was going back to heaven, to his Father's house. His disciples would be praying directly to the heavenly Father, and the Father would give to them in the name of his Son, just as if the Son himself were praying. If they asked in his name they would receive and would find full joy in receiving from God. Jesus said: "In that day you will ask in my name; and I do not say to you that I shall pray the Father for you; for the Father himself loves you, because you have loved me and have believed that I came from the Father" (vv. 26, 27). Jesus is telling them that when they ask God for something in the name of the Son, God will answer them directly without Jesus having to intercede on their behalf. God loved them and would answer them as they prayed in the name of Jesus.

Another condition that governs at least some of our prayers is agreement with other Christians about our petitions. So the Lord said, "Again I say to you, if two of you agree on earth about anything they ask, it will be done for them by my Father in heaven. For where two or three are gathered in my name, there am I in the midst of them" (Matt. 18:19, 20). If two Christians can come to a complete and honest agreement about anything they ask as they are gathered in his name, God will give it to them. This should encourage groups of Christians to pray together and to come to perfect unity of heart and mind as they make their requests to God. Jesus is always present when we are meeting on his behalf and for the good of his cause and are making our united prayers to the Father. This is as true of two or three hundred or two or three thousand, as it is of just two or three.

Believing is always a condition of effective praying.

You remember that when the barren fig tree withered at the word of Jesus his disciples were amazed, but the Master said to them, "Truly, I say to you, if you have faith and never doubt, you will not only do what has been done to the fig tree, but even if you say to this mountain, 'Be taken up and cast into the sea,' it will be done. And whatever you ask in prayer, you will receive, if you have faith" (Matt. 21:21, 22). Mountains of difficulty will be removed if we have faith, and such faith will enable us to receive what we ask for. Mark quotes Jesus on this occasion as saying, "Therefore I tell you, whatever you ask in prayer, believe that you receive it, and you will" (Mark 11:24). True faith and trust in God is a condition of effective prayer, for if we trust in our heavenly Father he will answer our prayers.

It stands to reason that our prayer must be in accordance with God's will. This is certainly an important condition of right praying. In our ignorance and stupidity and short-sightedness we often ask God for things that would be harmful and wrong for us, just as children often ask parents for things that are bad for them. A loving God would no more give bad things to his children than a loving parent on earth would knowingly give his child something that would be detrimental. In our praying we are, like Jesus, to pray, "Thy will be done." We must always make our prayers conform to the divine will.

Then Jesus teaches that he will also send the Holy Spirit of truth to be like him in guiding and teaching us: "But the Counselor, the Holy Spirit, whom the Father will send in my name, he will teach you all things, and bring to your remembrance all that I have said to you" (John 14:26). Again, Jesus said, "I have yet many things to say to you, but you cannot bear them now. When the Spirit of truth comes, he will guide you into all the truth; for he will not speak on his own authority, but whatever he hears he will speak, and he will declare to you the things that are to come. He will glorify me, for he will take what is mine and declare it to you" (John 16:12–14). The Holy Spirit helps us in our praying and guides us to pray in the right spirit.

The last condition of effective prayer is given in these words of our Lord: "If you abide in me, and my words abide in you, ask whatever you will, and it shall be done for you" (John 15:7). This means that if we live in Christ by faith and have his truth in our hearts and minds, then our prayers will answered for we shall not ask for anything contrary to his revealed truth or inconsistent with his indwelling presence.

Jesus tells us also where we are to pray: "But when you pray, go into your room and shut the door and pray to your Father who is in secret; and your Father who sees in secret will reward you" (Matt. 6:6). But not all of our praying is to be in secret. We have already seen that we are to be united with others in our prayers and are to gather in his name in groups to pray. His Father's house is "a house of prayer." We are to pray everywhere. Jesus told the Samaritan woman that God is spirit and so can be worshiped anywhere and everywhere.

What are we to pray for? We are to pray for "anything" (John 14:14) we think we need, for "all things," for our enemies, our persecutors, for those who despitefully use us, for the laborers in the Lord's harvest fields, for our daily bread, for the kingdom of God, for friends, for healing, for comfort, for power from on high—for anything under the sun that we believe is good and right.

When shall we pray? At any time. We shall see later

some of the occasions on which our Lord prayed. He sets no special hours for us. We are to pray always, and also at special times.

Why are we to pray? It is as natural for a child to pray to his heavenly Father as it is for him to make requests of his own parents. We are to pray when we want something; yes, of course we are; but we are to pray also when we just want to be in the divine presence. God knows what we need, but often we do not. We are not to "heap up empty phrases as the Gentiles do; for they think that they will be heard for their many words" (Matt. 6:7, 8). We are to pray, for the right sort of praying will do more to bless us and others than anything else we can do. We are to pray because, as Tennyson wrote:

> More things are wrought by prayer
> Than this world dreams of.
>
> —"Morte D'Arthur"

13

Purity and Vision

"Blessed are the pure in heart, for they shall see God" (Matt. 5:8).

Sometimes when we try to pray, we have a feeling that it is all in vain. We have neither seen God nor heard his voice. We come to the conclusion that something is wrong; and something surely is wrong! In Isaiah 59:1–3 we read:

> Behold, the Lord's hand is not shortened, that it cannot save, or his ear dull, that it cannot hear; but your iniquities have made a separation between you and your God, and your sins have hid his face from you so that he does not hear. For your hands are defiled with blood and your fingers with iniquity; your lips have spoken lies, your tongue mutters wickedness.

Then in Isaiah 1:15–17 we have these words:

> When you spread forth your hands, I will hide my eyes from you; even though you make many prayers, I will

> not listen; your hands are full of blood. Wash yourselves; make yourselves clean; remove the evil of your doings from before my eyes; cease to do evil, learn to do good; seek justice, correct oppression; defend the fatherless, plead for the widow.

So we come to the words of Jesus: "Blessed are the pure in heart, for they shall see God" (Matt. 5:8). These words give one of his clearest teachings on prayer. Can we see God? Have we ever seen him? The Bible says, "No one has ever seen God" (John 1:18; 1 John 4:12). And yet the Bible also speaks of seeing God. Many of the Old Testament saints walked and talked with him. He "appeared" to them in many ways. We read that Moses "endured as seeing him who is invisible" (Heb. 11:27). God had said to Moses: "You cannot see my face; for man shall not see me and live" (Exod. 33:20). Yet God said to him, "Behold, there is a place by me where you shall stand upon the rock; and while my glory passes by I will put you in a cleft of the rock, and I will cover you with my hand until I have passed by; then I will take away my hand, and you shall see my back; but my face shall not be seen" (vv. 21–23). Job cried, "I had heard of thee by the hearing of the ear, but now my eye sees thee" (Job 42:5). Jacob wrestled all night with "a man" (Gen. 32:24) and next morning he said, "For I have seen God face to face, and yet my life is preserved" (v. 30). Young Isaiah said, "In the year that king Uzziah died I saw the Lord sitting upon a throne, high and lifted up; and his train filled the temple" (Isa. 6:1). John in Revelation had visions of God upon his throne, but pictured him only in terms of light and radiant beauty and glory. This brings us back to the words of our Lord: "Blessed are the pure in heart, for they shall see God." We may conclude that we are indeed impure, for we have never truly seen God. We have tried to pray, but all seemed unreal and even hypocritical. So let us examine these words of our supreme authority and see if we can get help from them. What does the Bible mean by "seeing God"? What did Jesus mean by these words of our text?

Jesus tells us that it is only "the pure in heart" who "shall see God." The word "heart" is used in the Bible to include the mind, the will, the whole personality—not just the emotional nature. The psalmist asked and answered a pertinent question: "Who shall ascend the hill of the LORD? And who shall stand in his holy place? He who has clean hands and a pure heart, who does not lift up his soul to what is false, and does not swear deceitfully. He will receive blessing from the LORD, and vindication from the God of his salvation" (Ps. 24:3–5). James, the Lord's brother, wrote: "Draw near to God and he will draw near to you. Cleanse your hands, you sinners, and purify your hearts, you men of double mind" (James 4:8).

The word "pure" is used in the Bible to denote, first of all, that which is clean or free from dirt. It is used of things and of persons and includes physical and moral cleansing. To live a clean life is to live a life that is free from sin and all that defiles. The word "pure" is also used to denote wheat that was cleansed of chaff. John the Baptist spoke of Jesus whose "winnowing fork is in his hand, to clear his threshing floor, and to gather the wheat into his granary, but the chaff he will burn with unquenchable fire" (Luke 3:17). To cleanse means to get rid of the chaff, and it means to cleanse our life of sin and make it pure.

When something is "pure" it is the unadulterated article, free from alloys or dross, like gold that has been refined by the fire and cleansed of dross. The pure in heart are those who are altogether without hypocrisy, who have no mixed motives, who are not double-minded, who do not see with double vision, who do not wear spiritual bifocals. Jesus said in Matthew 6:22, "The eye is the lamp of the body. So, if your eye is sound, your whole body will be full of light; but if your eye is not sound, your whole body will be full of darkness." So "the pure in heart" are persons who have been cleansed of sin. They have a wholehearted love for Christ, a single devotion to the Lord, no mixed motives when they pray, and no double-mindedness. They do not seek to serve two masters. Their lives have been freed from impurity, selfishness, greed, and other sins. They have been purified by the Holy Spirit.

But how can we become pure in heart? David committed horrible sin and then he prayed for cleansing: "Wash me thoroughly from my iniquity, and cleanse me from my sin! Purge me with hyssop, and I shall be clean; wash me, and I shall be whiter than snow. Create in me a clean heart, O God, and put a new and right spirit within me" (Ps. 51:2, 7, 10). God said to the nation of Israel: "Come now, let us reason together . . . though your sins are like scarlet, they shall be as white as snow; though they are red like crimson, they shall become like wool" (Isa. 1:18). In First John 1:7 there is a relevant truth: "But if we walk in the light, as he is in the light, we have fellowship with one another, and the blood of Jesus his Son cleanses us from all sin." We also read, "If we confess our sins, he is faithful and just, and will forgive our sins and cleanse us from all unrighteousness" (v. 9). This teaching runs throughout the New Testament: true faith in the Son of God is what gives us a clean heart. Jesus said to his believing disciples: "You are already made clean by the word which I have spoken to you" (John 15:3). Paul wrote to his friends in Corinth, some of whom had been "immoral, idolaters, adulterers, homosexuals, thieves, greedy, drunkards, revilers, and robbers," and said to those who now believed in Christ: "But you were washed, you were sanctified, you were justified in the name of the Lord Jesus Christ and in the Spirit of our God" (1 Cor. 6:11). We become pure in heart as we trust in the Lord Jesus Christ who died on the cross and was raised from the dead for our cleaning from all sin.

Now Jesus promises that "the pure in heart . . . shall see God." What does he mean? He certainly does not mean that we shall see God with our physical eyes. Jesus also said, "God is spirit" (John 4:24), and we cannot see a spirit with our natural eyes. People did see Jesus, and he said, "He who has seen me has seen the Father" (John 14:9). And yet they did not see God by looking at the physical form of Jesus. Jesus is here saying that the heavenly Father is like the Son, and when we know Jesus as Savior, we know God. To see often means to understand. Someone tries to explain a big problem to us, and finally we cry out, "Oh, now I see! I see what you mean."

In what sense do the pure in heart see God? We see him in nature, in his universe: "The heavens are telling the glory of God; and the firmament proclaims his handiwork" (Ps. 19:1). We see him in the lovely flowers and blossoming plants in the springtime and in all the things God has made. We see God in the lives of people. His name is figuratively written on the foreheads of his redeemed. The pure in heart may reflect the image of God in their faces. We do see something of God in the faces of his true saints, in the faces of little children, sometimes in the faces of the sick, the suffering, and the needy.

We see God in the Bible. That is, we are aware of his presence as we read this holy book reverently with hungry hearts and open minds. As we walk through its pages we are walking with God and with his people. We see God in history, even as the prophets did. They were called seers because they could see God's hand in the events of the day. They saw the meaning and the purpose of history and were able to discern the signs of the times.

We see God in Jesus Christ. Paul called him "the image of the invisible God" (Col. 1:15), and the writer of Hebrews says he "reflects the glory of God and bears the very stamp of his nature" (Heb. 1:3). We see God in that we know he is like his Son Jesus Christ. We can see God in the sense that we can see the love of our parents. We do not see love with our natural eyes, but with our hearts. We do not see the air, but we breathe it.

Jesus was the perfect example of one who is pure in heart. This qualified him to see clearly, more clearly than any other. What did Jesus see? He saw the beauty of God's world, and it spoke to him of the heavenly Father. He observed the lilies of the field, the birds of the heavens, the mountains, the lakes, the trees, the sun and moon and stars. He saw the rain, the snow, the dewdrops. He saw God's signature written across the skies and his fingerprints upon the stars. Jesus saw the best in people, for he was always looking for the best. He saw their hearts and minds and knew what was in them. He saw their potentialities, what they might become when they were genuinely transformed by his Spirit.

Jesus saw sin and suffering—more clearly than any other person. He saw the hypocrisy of the Pharisees and the falseness of Herod and Pilate. He saw hidden motives and desires in human hearts. He saw the sick, the suffering, the needy. He saw clearly the meaning of history. He saw the coming of his Kingdom and his own coming on the clouds of glory. He saw God in all his universe: God's glory, beauty, goodness, and love! He was always conscious of the Father's presence and never felt alone. His purity gave him the clearest vision that any man ever had.

What will enable us to have a clearer vision of God? We have partially answered this question already. We must have purity of heart, single-minded devotion, and wholehearted love. We must "look ever to Jesus" and not to the things of the world. The person who is always looking at the things of the world and the pleasures of life only, has his eyes blinded by sin and the dazzling lights of the world. But purity enlightens one's vision, and faith enlarges it. Jesus spoke significant words to Martha as they came to the tomb of her dead brother: "Did I not tell you that if you would believe you would see the glory of God?" (John 11:40). Faith enables us to see the things that are spiritually discernible. The Holy Spirit will enlarge our vision as we receive him into our hearts. Paul prayed for the Ephesians: "That the God of our Lord Jesus Christ, the Father of glory, may give you a spirit of wisdom and of revelation in the knowledge of him, having the eyes of your hearts enlightened, that you may know what is the hope to which he has called you, what are the riches of his glorious inheritance in the saints" (Eph. 1:17, 18). John was "in the Spirit on the Lord's day" when he saw the glorious visions of God and of Christ upon the throne and when he saw the glories of heaven.

Walking in the light of Christ enables us to see clearly. Jesus said, "I am the light of the world; he who follows me will not walk in darkness, but will have the light of life" (John 8:12).

True worship enables us to see God. Young Isaiah had gone to the temple to worship when he had his visions of God upon his throne. John was worshiping when he had his revelations of God. Stephen was praying when he said, "Behold, I see the heavens opened, and the Son of man standing at the right hand of God" (Acts 7:56), and his vision enabled him to pray as he was being stoned to death, "Lord, do not hold this sin against them" (v. 60).

Christian service enables us to see God. We shall see God and Jesus in the faces of people whom we help. Jesus identifies himself with the hungry, the sick, the ill-clothed, the imprisoned, and the other needy ones. We can see him in their gratitude for our helpfulness.

One day we shall see God face to face. Paul said, "For now we see in a mirror dimly, but then face to face" (1 Cor. 13:12), and John declared, "We know that when he appears we shall be like him, for we shall see him as he is" (1 John 3:2). Jesus spoke of the day when "they will see the Son of man coming on the clouds of heaven with power and great glory" (Matt. 24:30). John wrote: "Behold, he is coming with the clouds, and every eye will see him" (Rev. 1:7).

Job cried out: "For I know that my Redeemer lives, and at last he will stand upon the earth; and after my skin has been thus destroyed, then from my flesh I shall see God, whom I shall see on my side, and my eyes shall behold, and not another" (Job 19:25–27).

Our praying will become more real and helpful when we become pure in heart and able to see God.

14

Christ's Authority in Prayer

"And Jesus came and said to them, 'All authority in heaven and on earth has been given to me'" (Matt. 28:18).

Maybe we do not at first think of this as a verse on prayer, but it has deep meaning in regard to prayer and shows us much about the teaching of our Lord on this subject. The risen Lord said this and then immediately added, "And lo, I am with you always, to the close of the age" (Matt. 28:20). Jesus also tells us that the Son "can do nothing of his own accord" (John 5:19), but that the Father loves the Son and shares with him his power to raise the dead and to do all things, and then he declares, "The Father judges no one, but has given all judgment to the Son" (v. 22). In John 14:6 Jesus states a relevant truth: "I am the way, and the truth, and the life; no one comes to the Father, but by me." Then in Matthew 11:27 he says: "All things have been delivered to me by my Father; and no one knows the Son except the Father, and no one knows the Father except the Son and any one to whom the Son chooses to reveal him." The point we are getting at is that Jesus teaches that he has full authority to hear and answer all our prayers, that he is always present with his people through the Holy Spirit, that we can come directly to him in prayer and that he will hear and answer us. Some of us may think that we have to go directly to God the Father, in our praying, but we can go directly to Jesus Christ who has full authority to answer us and to give us what we request.

Stephen, the first Christian martyr, prayed directly to the Lord Jesus Christ, saying, "Lord Jesus, receive my spirit" (Acts 7:59), and again, "Lord, do not hold this sin against them" (v. 60). Sometimes we cannot be sure whether the prayers of Paul were addressed to God the Father or to the Lord Jesus; for example, Paul prayed to "the Lord" about his thorn in the flesh, and the Lord said to him, "My grace is sufficient for you, for my power is made perfect in weakness" (2 Cor. 12:9), and in the same verse Paul declared, "I will all the more gladly boast of my weaknesses, that the power of Christ may rest upon me." This would indicate that he was praying directly to Christ.

During his public ministry Jesus answered many prayers and invited the people to come to God through him. He said, "Come to me, all who labor and are heavy laden, and I will give you rest. . . . and you will find rest for your souls" (Matt. 11:28, 29).

It may help us to look at some prayers that Jesus answered by giving the person what he prayed for or earnestly desired. Some of these may not sound like prayers for they may not be expressed in the accustomed forms of prayer; but they were prayers in the sense that they represented the real desire and longing of the person for divine help.

At the wedding in Cana of Galilee when the wine failed, the mother of Jesus came to him, saying, "They have no wine" (John 2:3). She had doubtless gone to her son with many problems before, knowing that he would help her. Here Jesus performed his first miracle in answer to the prayer of his mother.

When four friends brought a paralytic to Jesus to be healed, they did not make a formal prayer asking Jesus to heal the man, but they prayed by their faith and their action. The crowd was so large in the house where Jesus was preaching that they could not enter by the door; so they went up the outside steps and lifted some tiles from the roof and let down their friend into the room where Jesus was. "And when Jesus saw their faith, he said to the paralytic, 'My son, your sins are forgiven'" (Mark 2:5). Their real desire was for this man to be healed of his paralysis, and they had faith to believe that Jesus could and would heal him. Jesus more than answered their prayer: he forgave the young man of his sins. That was the man's first need, and Jesus met that need and demonstrated his "authority on earth to forgive sins" (v. 10) by healing the man. The people "were all amazed and glorified God, saying, 'We never saw anything like this!'" (v. 12).

Mark tells us in his very first chapter that Jesus cast out an unclean spirit from a man in the synagogue, and the people asked, "What is this? A new teaching! With authority he commands even the unclean spirits, and they obey him" (v. 27). Mark goes on to say: "And a leper came to him beseeching him, and kneeling said to him, 'If you will, you can make me clean.' Moved with pity, he stretched out his hand and touched him, and said to him, 'I will; be clean.' And immediately the leprosy left him, and he was made clean" (vv. 40–42).

Mark also tells of Jesus raising the little daughter of Jairus from the dead. Jairus, a ruler of the synagogue, came to Jesus, and fell at his feet, beseeching him, "My little daughter is at the point of death. Come and lay your hands on her, so that she may be made well, and live" (Mark 5:23). Jesus went home with this Jewish ruler and found that the little twelve-year-old girl had died. Jesus went into the room and took the dead child by the hand, saying, "'Tálitha cúmi'; which means, 'Little girl, I say to you, arise'. And immediately the girl got up and walked; for she was twelve years old" (vv. 41, 42).

As Jesus was on his way to the house of Jairus a large crowd followed him. Mark tells us of a woman who had suffered with a hemorrhage for twelve years and was humanly incurable. She came up and tried to touch the robe of Jesus secretly, for she said, "If I touch even his garments, I shall be made well" (v. 28). She was immediately healed. When Jesus had asked who touched him, the woman "knowing what had been done to her, came in fear and trembling and fell down before him, and told him the whole truth. And he said to her, 'Daughter, your faith has made you well; go in peace, and be healed of your disease'" (vv. 33, 34). Maybe this was not the kind of formal prayer we might hear on Sunday morning in a church, but it was real praying nonetheless. There was sincere, intense desire for help, and a complete telling of the truth, and the Lord fully answered her prayer.

You recall that when Jesus was praying on the mount where he was transfigured, nine of his disciples were down in the valley vainly trying to heal the epileptic son of a man who had brought him for healing. These disciples failed because of their "little faith" (Matt. 17:20). Then when the man saw Jesus approaching, the "man came up to him and kneeling before him said, 'Lord, have mercy on my son, for he is an epileptic and he suffers terribly; for often he falls into the fire, and often into the water. And I brought him to your disciples, and they could not heal him'" (vv. 14–16). Jesus immediately healed the boy and gave him back to his father. This was the occasion on which Jesus said to his disciples, "For truly, I say to you, if you have faith as a grain of mustard seed, you will say to this mountain, 'Move hence to yonder place,' and it will move; and nothing will be impossible to you" (v. 20)

Luke tells us of the Roman centurion who had a slave he loved dearly. The slave was sick and "at the point of death." This army officer sent some of his Jewish friends to Jesus with the prayer that he come and heal the boy. "And when they came to Jesus, they besought him earnestly, saying, 'He is worthy to have you do this for him, for he loves our nation, and he built us our synagogue'" (Luke 7:4, 5). When Jesus approached the house of the military officer, the man sent other friends to him and said,

> "Lord, do not trouble yourself, for I am not worthy to have you come under my roof; therefore I did not presume to come to you. But say the word, and let my servant be healed." When Jesus heard this he marveled at him, and turned and said to the multitude that followed him, "I tell you, not even in Israel have I found such faith." (vv. 6, 7, 9)

The slave was immediately healed, and it was in answer to prayer.

Matthew tells us of the Canaanite woman from the region of Tyre and Sidon who came to Jesus as he was in that vicinity and prayed, "Have mercy on me, O Lord, Son of David; my daughter is severely possessed by a demon" (Matt. 15:22). At first Jesus seemed to pay no attention to her and did not answer her immediately. His disciples requested that she be sent away for they considered her a nuisance. Jesus said to her, "I was sent only to the lost sheep of the house of Israel" (v. 24). But as she knelt before him she cried, "Lord, help me" (v. 25). That was real prayer. Jesus may have been testing her faith, or he may have been teaching his disciples a lesson on racial prejudice when he answered, "It is not fair to take the children's bread and throw it to the dogs" (v. 26). That does not sound at all like Jesus. We might better understand him if we could have seen the expression on his face as he spoke. I believe that the woman saw and understood, for she persisted, saying, "Yes, Lord, yet even the dogs eat the crumbs that fall from their master's table" (v. 27). Then Jesus said something that he never said to any other woman, so far as the New Testament record tells us, "O woman, great is your faith! Be it done for you as you desire" (v. 28). This event certainly contains a lesson on prayer.

On and on we could go through the Gospels, showing how Jesus answered every sincere prayer for help. Even on the cross the robber crucified by his side prayed, "Jesus, remember me when you come in your kingly power." Though he was dying, Jesus took time to answer this prayer of a repenting sinner with a glorious truth, "Truly, I say to you, today you will be with me in Paradise" (Luke 23:42, 43).

But Jesus did not always say yes to all who made requests of him. Sometimes he said no. He said no to all insincere, selfish, and unworthy prayers. He said no to James and John and their ambitious mother. Matthew tells us that the mother, along with her two sons, came and knelt before Jesus. He asked her what she wanted. "She said to him, 'Command that these two sons of mine may sit, one at your right hand and one at your left, in your kingdom'" (Matt. 20:21). Observe very carefully the reply of Jesus: "'You do not know what you are asking. Are you able to drink the cup that I am to drink?' They said to him, 'We are able.' He said to them, 'You will drink my cup, but to sit at my right hand and at my left is not mine to grant, but it is for those for whom it has been prepared by my Father'" (vv. 22, 23). This wrong sort of praying was not only rebuked by Jesus, but it made the other disciples "indignant." How many times could Jesus say to us, "You do not know what you are asking?"

On another occasion Jesus rebuked these same two close friends for asking for permission to pray for God to send fire from heaven and burn up the hostile village that would not give overnight accommodations to them (Luke 9:51–55).

Jesus also denied the request of a covetous man who came to him, saying, "Teacher, bid my brother divide the inheritance with me" (Luke 12:13). Jesus said to him, "Man, who made me a judge or divider over you?" (v. 14). Then Jesus turned to the whole crowd and to his own disciples, "Take heed, and beware of all covetousness; for a man's life does not consist in the abundance of his possessions" (v. 15). Jesus denied this request because the man's motives were wrong. He was filled with greed, selfishness, covetousness, and unbrotherliness—all signs of a materialistic view of life. If Jesus had acted as judge here, he probably would have caused hard feelings in this family. Perhaps both brothers were guilty. Jesus still says no to our prayers that have the wrong motive or are made in the wrong spirit.

Our Lord also said no to a cured demoniac. This man had been a raving lunatic, living in the cemeteries and caves, wearing no clothes, a terror to the whole neighborhood. But Jesus healed the man and brought him back to sanity and to a place in society. This cured man was grateful to Jesus and begged that he might accompany him; but Jesus said to him, "Go home to your friends, and tell them how much the Lord has done for you, and how he has had mercy on you" (Mark 5:19). This man was refused his request, but he was given an important task. "And he went away and began to proclaim in the Decapólis how much Jesus had done for him; and all men marveled" (v. 20). He recognized Jesus as the Lord and told others about him.

Jesus denied the requests of the religious authorities who asked him for a sign from heaven and the requests of those who asked him to explain by what authority he did his preaching and work. He said to them: "An evil and adulterous generation seeks for a sign; but no sign shall be given to it except the sign of the prophet Jonah. For as Jonah was three days and three nights in the belly of the whale, so will the Son of man be three days and three nights in the heart of the earth" (Matt. 12:39, 40). When the religious leaders asked him,

> "By what authority are you doing these things, and who gave you this authority?" Jesus answered them, "I also will ask you a question; and if you tell me the answer, then I also will tell you by what authority I do these things. The baptism of John, whence was it?

From heaven or from men?" And they argued with one another, "If we say, 'From heaven,' he will say to us, 'Why then did you not believe him?' But if we say, 'From men,' we are afraid of the multitude; for all hold that John was a prophet." So they answered Jesus, "We do not know." And he said to them, "Neither will I tell you by what authority I do these things." (Matt. 21:23–27)

The religious authorities could not answer Jesus' question without being caught on the horns of a dilemma, so when they confessed their ignorance Jesus was free to declare that he had no reason to answer the question they had put to him.

Jesus will deny the request of some people on the Judgment Day. He declared in his Sermon on the Mount,

> "Not every one who says to me, 'Lord, Lord,' shall enter the kingdom of heaven, but he who does the will of my Father who is in heaven. On that day many will say to me, 'Lord, Lord, did we not prophesy in your name, and cast out demons in your name, and do many mighty works in your name?' And then will I declare to them, 'I never knew you; depart from me, you evildoers.'" (Matt. 7:21–23)

On that day it will be too late to pray, "Lord, lord, open to us . . ." for he will say, "Truly, I say to you, I do not know you" (Matt. 25:11, 12).

Yes, Jesus has "all authority in heaven and on earth." He has authority to grant or to refuse any prayers that are made to him. He is by the side of every believer all the way and will answer every sincere prayer; but he will deny every insincere, unworthy and wrong request.

The Lord to whom we pray has made this glorious promise: "All that the Father gives me will come to me; and him who comes to me I will not cast out" (John 6:37).

PART TWO

"Pray as I Pray"

15

A Look at Jesus Praying

"As he was praying . . ." (Luke 9:18).

In Part One we have been studying what Jesus said about prayer. Now in Part Two we will observe Jesus himself as he prays. Where, when, what, and why did he pray? Part 1 was, "Pray as I Say," and now in Part Two Jesus is saying in effect, "Pray as I Pray." We can learn much about prayer by watching Jesus as he communes with God.

The Gospels mention many occasions when Jesus prayed. He prayed at his baptism. "Now when all the people were baptized, and when Jesus also had been baptized and was praying, the heaven was opened, and the Holy Spirit descended upon him in bodily form, as a dove, and a voice came from heaven, 'Thou art my beloved Son; with thee I am well pleased'" (Luke 3:21, 22). Jesus was praying on this occasion as he was beginning his great public ministry. This was a time of special dedication to God. He made a complete commitment, a full surrender, and prayed for God's blessings on the work he was setting out to accomplish.

This incident shows something of the seriousness of baptism. It should always be done in a reverent spirit and in a manner pleasing to God. It was a symbol of the fulfillment of all righteousness.

Something happened as Jesus prayed on this occasion: the Holy Spirit descended upon him "in bodily form, as a dove." The Holy Spirit was always present with Jesus, filling him, guiding him, and empowering him. "And Jesus, full of the Holy Spirit, returned from the Jordan, and was led by the Spirit . . ." (Luke 4:1). We see that the Spirit came in a visible form at the beginning of his ministry. It is very significant to notice that as Jesus prayed the Spirit came and God answered from heaven in a very definite and unmistakable way, saying, "Thou art my beloved Son; with thee I am well pleased."

Surely it is reasonable to believe that Jesus prayed during his threefold temptation. The Gospels do not give us the definite words of Jesus' prayer, but the whole experience was certainly one in which there was much prayer and meditation, for Jesus was mapping out his public ministry. The devil suggested that he use the methods of the world, that he use his supernatural powers to satisfy his hunger, that he solve the economic problem by providing bread—and if bread, then all material needs—for the benefit of men. The people would follow him if he would put "a chicken in every pot" or bring financial prosperity to all. Jesus reminded Satan that the Scriptures commanded man to live, not by the material alone, but by the spiritual: by "every word that proceeds from the mouth of God" (Matt. 4:4). It was certainly while Jesus prayed that he came to this decision or confirmed a previous decision that his ministry would be spiritual, not material. He would not neglect bread for the hungry, but he would later tell the people: "Do not labor for the food which perishes, but for the food which endures to eternal life, which the Son of man will give to you; for on him has God the Father set his seal" (John 6:27).

Jesus was surely praying when the devil suggested that he worship him in exchange for the worldly kingdoms and their glory. Jesus was worshiping God, and the devil was jealous. Jesus was praying to his Father, and the devil wanted him to pray to "his Satanic majesty." Jesus quoted the Scriptures to Satan, "You shall worship the Lord your God, and him only shall you serve" (Luke 4:8). It was as he prayed that he dedicated himself and his ministry to God and his eternal truth with absolutely no compromise with the devil.

Then the devil suggested that he make a spectacular display of his supernatural power and God's protecting love by leaping from the pinnacle of the temple as the curious and applauding crowds watched in amazement. It was a temptation to win popular support and acclaim by sensational and spectacular means. Jesus again quoted the Scriptures: "You shall not tempt the Lord your God" (v. 12).

This took place during a period of forty days in the wilderness. It is unthinkable to suppose that Jesus did not pray on this occasion. He was not alone, as he said later, "I am not alone, for the Father is with me" (John 16:32). The entire temptation experience was steeped in earnest prayer. Jesus won victories that only prayer can win. After the devil left him we know that "Angels came and ministered to him" (Matt. 4:11).

Mark points to what was doubtless a habit of Jesus: "And in the morning, a great while before day, he rose and went out to a lonely place, and there he prayed"

(Mark 1:35). And Luke gives an even more remarkable picture of Jesus as a man of prayer: "In these days he went out into the hills to pray; and all night he continued in prayer to God" (Luke 6:12). Sometimes we wake up in the middle of the night and find it difficult to go back to sleep. That is a good time to pray, but Jesus spent the entire night in prayer. What was the burden of his prayer? The answer is suggested in the next verse, "And when it was day, he called his disciples, and chose from them twelve, whom he named apostles" (v. 13). He was selecting the twelve men upon whom he would depend for help in his work in the world. It was certainly not the list that any of us would have chosen, but it was the right list. He even chose Judas Iscariot! Why? Who can say? But Judas could have been different if only he had followed the Master, for he—like other men—had freedom of will.

Luke tells us concerning Jesus, "He was praying in a certain place, and when he ceased, one of his disciples said to him, 'Lord, teach us to pray, as John taught his disciples'" (Luke 11:1). They were so impressed with his praying that they wanted to know more about the secret of its effectiveness. We have already studied his answer to that request: It was the model prayer, the Lord's Prayer.

Jesus was praying near Caesarea Philippi when Peter made his great confession. "Now it happened that as he was praying alone the disciples were with him; and he asked them, 'Who do the people say that I am?'" (Luke 9:18). They reported that some thought he was John the Baptist or Elijah or another of the old prophets come back to life. When he asked, "But who do you say that I am?" Peter answered, "The Christ of God" (v. 20). Matthew reports that Peter said, "You are the Christ, the Son of the living God" (Matt. 16:16).

Jesus acknowledged the insight and reminded Peter that God had made this special revelation to him.

Jesus prayed on the Mount of Transfiguration. He took "with him Peter and John and James, and went up on the mountain to pray" (Luke 9:28). Note carefully that he did not go to be transfigured, but to pray. Luke tells us, "As he was praying" he was transfigured.

Jesus also prayed in the presence of death (John 11:41); he prayed before meals; he prayed when little children were brought to him for his blessing (Matt. 19:13); he prayed in the garden of Gethsemane. On the cross he prayed at least three prayers, which we shall study in a separate chapter. His longest prayer recorded in the Gospels is found in John 17. Jesus said to Peter when he tried to defend him with the sword, "Put your sword back into its place; for all who take the sword will perish by the sword. Do you think that I cannot appeal to my Father, and he will at once send me more than twelve legions of angels?" (Matt. 26:52, 53).

On the night before his death he said to his disciples: "And I will pray the Father, and he will give you another Counselor, to be with you for ever, even the Spirit of truth, whom the world cannot receive, because it neither sees him nor knows him; you know him, for he dwells with you, and will be in you" (John 14:16, 17).

Jesus said that God the Father revealed truth to him: "For I have not spoken on my own authority; the Father who sent me has himself given me commandment what to say and what to speak. . . . What I say, therefore, I say as the Father has bidden me" (John 12:49, 50).

Let us look very briefly at some of the short prayers of Jesus. He prayed before meals. When he fed the five thousand, he "looked up to heaven, and blessed, and broke and gave the loaves to the disciples, and the disciples gave them to the crowds" (Matt. 14:19). When he fed the four thousand he "took the seven loaves and the fish, and having given thanks" he gave the food to them (Matt. 15:36). He blessed the bread and the wine at the first Lord's Supper (Matt. 26:26, 27). The risen Lord was in the home of two disciples in Emmaus, and "When he was at table with them, he took the bread and blessed, and broke it, and gave it to them" (Luke 24:30). They recognized him by his breaking of bread and giving thanks (v. 35).

Jesus prayed for Simon Peter on that tragic night and said to him, "Simon, Simon, behold, Satan demanded to have you, that he might sift you like wheat, but I have prayed for you that your faith may not fail; and when you have turned again, strengthen your brethren" (Luke 22:31, 32).

Earlier in his ministry he prayed, "I thank thee, Father, Lord of heaven and earth, that thou hast hidden these things from the wise and understanding and revealed them to babes; yea, Father, for such was thy gracious will" (Matt. 11:25, 26). He went on to say that God had delivered all things to him, including the exclusive power to reveal God to others (v. 27).

By the tomb of Lazarus, who had been dead four days, Jesus prayed: "Father, I thank thee that thou hast heard me. I knew that thou hearest me always, but I have said this on account of the people standing by, that they may believe that thou didst send me" (John 11:41, 42). Jesus had already prayed about raising Lazarus from the dead, and here he was thanking God for hearing that prayer and for the assurance that God would do as Jesus had asked him. Then he said that he knew that God always heard his prayers. What a blessed assurance that was!

One of our Lord's briefest prayers was followed by a dramatic response:

> "Now is my soul troubled. And what shall I say? 'Father, save me from this hour'? No, for this purpose I have come to this hour. Father, glorify thy name." Then a voice came from heaven, "I have glorified it, and I will glorify it again." The crowd standing by heard it and said that it had thundered. Others said, "An angel has spoken to him." Jesus answered, "This voice has come for your sake, not for mine. Now is the judgment of this world, now shall the ruler of this world be cast out; and I, when I am lifted up from the earth, will draw all men to myself." (John 12:27–32)

The passages from the Gospels show that Jesus was truly a man of prayer. "As he was praying" many things took place. What happens when we pray?

16

Prayer and Transfiguration

"And he was transfigured before them, and his face shone like the sun, and his garments became white as light" (Matt. 17:2).

Does anything happen when we pray? Sometimes when we try to pray it seems that nothing at all happens. Things are just the same, and we may think that it makes no difference whether we pray or not.

But something took place when Jesus prayed. It was about six months before his crucifixion when he was transfigured. Jesus did not go up on the mountain to be transfigured, but, as Luke tells us, he "went up on the mountain to pray" (Luke 9:28). "And as he was praying, the appearance of his countenance was altered, and his raiment became dazzling white" (v. 29). Matthew, Mark, and Luke all give us the accounts of the transfiguration of our Lord. John is referring to it when he writes, "And the Word became flesh and dwelt among us, full of grace and truth; we have beheld his glory, glory as of the only Son from the Father" (John 1:14).

The transfiguration probably took place on the slopes of Mount Hermon, a snowcapped mountain over nine thousand feet high. Such a majestic setting was fitting for this significant event. Jesus had just told his disciples for the first time of his approaching crucifixion. At Caesarea Philippi he had asked his disciples, "Who do men say that the Son of man is?" (Matt. 16:13), and they gave various answers. When he asked who they thought he was, Peter said, "You are the Christ, the Son of the living God" (v. 16). God himself had revealed this truth to Simon Peter. Matthew then tells us: "From that time Jesus began to show his disciples that he must go to Jerusalem and suffer many things from the elders and chief priests and scribes, and be killed, and on the third day be raised" (v. 21). Peter said, "God forbid, Lord! This shall never happen to you" (v. 22). There was no cross in the theology of Simon Peter at that time, as there is no cross in the theology of many people today. But Jesus rebuked Peter and told his disciples, "If any man would come after me, let him deny himself and take up his cross and follow me" (v. 24). Then he told them that "the Son of man is to come with his angels in the glory of his Father" (v. 27). It was about a week later when Jesus took three of his dearest and closest disciples with him and "went up on the mountain to pray" (Luke 9:28), and the transfiguration occurred. This event reveals much about our blessed Lord.

It indicates something about his prayer life. Jesus often prayed to his Father. In fact, he was always aware of the living presence of God and was in constant communion and communication with him. He had a hot line direct to God's throne of grace. Jesus prayed early in the morning before daybreak. At least once he prayed all night long: "In these days he went out into the hills to pray; and all night he continued in prayer to God" (Luke 6:12). He prayed before every great decision, as for example when he chose his twelve apostles (v. 13). It seems that Jesus loved to go up into the hills to pray, for their majestic glory and magnificent beauty reminded him of the glory and the beauty of his God and Father. It was a quiet place, a place where there would be no interruptions.

Now we can pray in any place and at any time, as Jesus told the woman of Samaria: "Woman, believe me, the hour is coming when neither on this mountain nor in Jerusalem will you worship the Father. But the hour is coming, and now is, when the true worshippers will worship the Father in spirit and truth, for such the Father seeks to worship him. God is spirit, and those who worship him must worship in spirit and truth" (John 4:21, 23, 24). Jesus told his disciples, "But when you pray, go into your room and shut the door and pray to your Father who is in secret; and your Father who sees in secret will reward you" (Matt. 6:6).

And yet God may seem nearer on a mountaintop than he does in some other place. It was on Mount Sinai that God spoke to Moses and gave him the Ten Commandments. It was there that Moses also had a transfiguration experience. "When Moses came down from Mount Sinai, with the two tables of the testimony in his hand as he came down from the mountain, Moses did not know that the skin of his face shone because he had been talking with God" (Exod. 34:29). Real communion with God makes one's face radiant with divine glory.

What did Jesus pray about on the mountaintop? He prayed about his coming crucifixion, his resurrection, and his exodus from the world. The temptation to avoid the cross, had come at the beginning of his ministry, to win the world by compromising with the devil. This same suggestion had just come again through Simon Peter. This is why Jesus had spoken sharply to Simon: "Get behind me, Satan! You are a hindrance to me; for you are not on the side of God, but of men" (Matt. 16:23). Peter had man's outlook, not God's. Jesus needed to commit himself again to God and to dedicate himself completely to the doing of the Father's will. He wanted to reassure himself that the cross was in the plan of God. Could there be any doubt about it? We must remember that Jesus was human as well as divine, and as a human being he did not exactly relish the pain of the cross. He must have prayed for several hours, for Peter, James, and John were so sleepy that they found it difficult to stay awake. Here Jesus made a firm and complete recommitment and absolute surrender to God and his plan of salvation for man's redemption from sin. He prayed about this again on the night before his crucifixion, but there again he gave himself to the doing of God's will.

What happened as Jesus prayed? "And as he was praying, that appearance of his countenance was altered, and his raiment became dazzling white" (Luke 9:29). "He was transfigured before them, and his garments became glistening, intensely white, as no fuller on earth could bleach them" (Mark 9:2, 3). Matthew adds something significant to Mark's account: "And he was transfigured before them, and his face shone like the sun, and his garments became white as light" (Matt. 17:2). This happened as he communed with his Father.

It is such praying that brings a radiant and glorious countenance. As we saw, this was true when Moses prayed. Centuries later Stephen prayed and preached, "And gazing at him, all who sat in the council saw that his face was like the face of an angel" (Acts 6:15). Paul the apostle wrote: "And we all, with unveiled face, beholding the glory of the Lord, are being changed into his likeness from one degree of glory to another; for this comes from the Lord who is the Spirit" (2 Cor. 3:18).

Jesus had chosen his three closest friends, Peter, James, and John to go with him up the mountain. They needed this experience. Peter especially needed it, for he had remonstrated with Jesus about the cross. He needed to see the cross in a different light, as a thing of glory, not a badge of defeat or gloom. He needed to see it in the light of the resurrection and eternal salvation for all believers. Later Peter recalled this experience and wrote: "We were eyewitnesses of his majesty. For when he received honor and glory from God the Father and the voice was borne to him by the Majestic Glory, 'This is my beloved Son, with whom I am well pleased,' we heard this voice borne from heaven, for we were with him on the holy mountain" (2 Peter 1:16–18).

James needed this experience, for he was to be the first of the Twelve to become a martyr to the Christian faith. It would be easier to face death if he saw the glory that lay beyond.

John needed this experience. He was closest to Jesus in understanding and love, and would be best able to interpret the meaning and the glory of the cross and resurrection. He did this in his Gospel.

Jesus needed these human companions—dear friends who would be very close to him in this wonderful hour, who could share something of this marvelous experience. They were weak and frail and sleepy-headed; yet they loved him and would one day understand this experience.

Jesus had some heavenly companions too. Moses, the representative of the law, "appeared in glory and spoke of his departure, which he was to accomplish at Jerusalem" (Luke 9:31). As Moses had led the children out of Egyptian bondage, so Jesus would lead all God's children out of the bondage of sin. He was joined also by Elijah, the representative of the prophets, who had gone up to heaven in the first "space ship" (2 Kings 2:11). He could talk with Jesus about the glories of going to heaven. Of course, God was there, and he spoke, as we shall see in a moment.

What was the meaning of this transfiguration experience that came "as he was praying?" It revealed the truth that Jesus was full of grace and glory. The light came from within himself, from his own glorious person, not from the outside. "His face shone like the sun," says Matthew (17:2). Even his garments were whiter than any modern detergent could possibly get them. He is the source and origin of light. The Bible says, "God is light and in him is no darkness at all" (1 John 1:5). Jesus said, "I am the light of the world; he who follows me will not walk in darkness, but will have the light of life" (John 8:12). He was "transfigured" or metamorphosed. His clothing "became white as light" (Matt. 17:2), "dazzling white" (Luke 9:29). It was the light of his own glorious, sinless, holy, righteous, obedient life shining through.

Some day, according to the apostle Paul, the Lord Jesus will come from heaven and "will change our lowly body to be like his glorious body, by the power which enables him even to subject all things to himself" (Phil. 3:21).

The transfiguration signified victory to Jesus. He

had gained victory over sin. He had brought victory over death for others, and he would gain the victory over the death of the cross. It was God's pledge of victory, which would come on that resurrection morning about six months later when two men "in dazzling apparel" would say to some of the women, "Why do you seek the living among the dead?" (Luke 24:4, 5). Mary would find "two angels in white" sitting by the empty tomb, where the body of Jesus had been, but from which he had risen with a glorified body (John 20:12). This transfiguration experience would show the victory of Jesus over suffering. It would enable him "for the joy that was set before him" to endure the cross (Heb. 12:2). It would show his victory over death. Moses and Elijah were not dead. This foretaste of victory prepared Jesus for his cross.

It meant God's complete approval of his Son. Peter wanted to stay on the mountain to continue to enjoy this glorious experience; and he offered to build three booths for Jesus, Moses, and Elijah. He and James and John were not included in this suggestion. They would be happy just to be present out under the stars or at the feet of these three. But as Peter was speaking, "A bright cloud overshadowed them, and a voice from the cloud said, 'This is my beloved Son, with whom I am well pleased; listen to him'" (Matt. 17:5). This voice meant much to Jesus, for it showed God's complete love and approval of his Son. God was with him and would be with him all the way. God was not to forsake his Son but was to be "in Christ reconciling the world to himself" (2 Cor. 5:19).

This experience meant much to the disciples. Afterward they would never doubt the divine nature of Jesus. They saw him as sinless, majestic, glorious, and victorious. They did not fully grasp this at the time, but they would begin to understand it more after the crucifixion and the resurrection. It meant that Jesus was God's "Word become flesh," and they were to "listen to him." They would henceforth sit at his feet and hear his words. Peter had said, "Lord, to whom shall we go? You have the words of eternal life; and we have believed, and have come to know, that you are the Holy One of God" (John 6:68, 69).

What does this event mean to us today? It means that Jesus is all he claimed to be, God's glorious Son and man's victorious Savior, full of grace and glory. It should show us that something really does happen when we pray sincerely. It will transform us and cause our personalities to be radiant as we live in the presence of God.

17

A Prayer for Divine Glory

"Father, the hour has come; glorify thy Son that the Son may glorify thee" (John 17:1).

This is the Lord's Prayer, par excellence, the prayer that the Lord himself prayed. It is the longest of his prayers recorded in the Gospels. The key word in it is "glory," or some form of this word. Jesus uses it eight times here. It is the Glory, Glory, Hallelujah prayer that Jesus prayed before entering the garden of Gethsemane on the night before his crucifixion. It may be called his high priestly prayer. Let us now listen reverently as Jesus prays for himself, for his apostles, and even for us.

He prays for himself (John 17:1–5); the Son is here talking with the Father. The word "Father" occurs six times here. Jesus calls God, Holy Father (v. 11), righteous Father (v. 25), and simply Father four times. He calls himself the Son and refers five times to the fact that God sent him.

"Father, the hour has come," the hour he had seen from the beginning, the hour for which he had come into the world. Early in his ministry, at the wedding in Cana of Galilee he had said to his mother, "My hour has not yet come" (John 2:4). John tells us that once "they sought to arrest him; but no one laid hands on him, because his hour had not yet come" (John 7:30). Later he said, "The hour has come for the Son of man to be glorified" (John 12:23); and again, "'Now is my soul troubled. And what shall I say? "Father, save me from this hour"? No, for this purpose I have come to this hour. Father, glorify thy name.' Then a voice came from heaven, 'I have glorified it, and I will glorify it again'" (John 12:27, 28). In John 13:1 we read, "Now before the feast of the Passover, when Jesus knew that his hour had come to depart out of this world to the Father, having loved his own who were in the world, he loved them to the end." In the garden of Gethsemane he prayed "that, if it were possible, the hour might pass from him" (Mark 14:35). He is praying in the shadow of the cross, and he prays for divine glory: "Glorify thy Son that the Son may glorify thee" (John 17:1). The word "glorify" means to honor, to make radiant, to make beautiful, to exalt, to make splendid and majestic. This was no selfish prayer, for he desired his own glory only as a means to the Father's glory. The glorification of the Father was the one great desire of the Son. Here he says, "I glorified thee on the earth, having accomplished the work which thou gavest me to do" (v. 4). Jesus glorified God by faithfully doing his work and will in the world, by perfect obedience, by fidelity. Through the cross Jesus would bring "eternal life" (v. 2) to all believers the life that is found in the knowledge of the only true God and his Son, the Messiah, whom God had sent. This would be the saving knowledge, that Paul was to find in Christ (Phil 3:10, 11)."

Jesus prays, "And now, Father, glorify thou me in thy own presence with the glory which I had with thee before the world was made" (John 17:5). God would glorify Jesus upon the cross and then by his bodily resurrection from the dead. The Father would restore him to his place in heaven where they had shared divine glory before the creation of the world.

This prayer for glory was answered; for God glorified himself and his Son upon the cross, demonstrating divine love for all men everywhere, having made reconciliation, atonement for sin, and having provided eternal salvation. No wonder we sing, "In the Cross of Christ I Glory." God restored his Son to his former glory. Paul wrote of this in Philippians:

> And being found in human form he humbled himself and became obedient unto death, even death on a cross. Therefore God has highly exalted him and bestowed on him the name which is above every name, that at the name of Jesus every knee should bow, in heaven and on earth and under the earth, and every tongue confess that Jesus Christ is Lord, to the glory of God the Father. (2:8–11)

So here Jesus is praying for divine glory.

Next Jesus prayed for his disciples (John 17:6–19). Notice his generous attitude toward them: "They have kept thy word" (v. 6). They had been very weak and faulty, had quarreled among themselves, manifesting selfishness and personal ambition; and yet Jesus says that they had kept God's word. They had accepted the gospel, although as yet they did not understand it very clearly. Again, they knew that Jesus had come from God, and they had received his truth.

> Now they know that everything that thou hast given me is from thee; for I have given them the words which thou gavest me, and they have received them and know in truth that I came from thee; and they have believed that thou didst send me. I am praying for them . . . for those whom thou hast given me, for they are thine; and thine are mine and all mine are thine, I am glorified in them." (vv. 7, 8, 9, 10).

They all belonged to God in Christ, because they had believed on Christ and received God through him. "And I am glorified in them" (v. 10). In spite of their shortcomings and weaknesses, they had glorified Christ, at times anyway, and he was glad.

Here Jesus makes five petitions for these disciples.

First, he prays: "Keep them in thy name" (v. 11). Christ had kept them and guarded them and, except for Judas the betrayer, they were safe. Jesus had manifested God's name, or very nature, to them. He had demonstrated the true character of God in his own life. He had told them earlier that very night, "He who has seen me has seen the Father" (John 14:9). He had faithfully given them God's truth, and they had received it. The world hated them because they were different. They might be tempted to hate back. Jesus was leaving them for a little while, and true to the divine character, he prays to his Father, "Keep them in thy name."

Then he prays "that they may be one, even as we are one" (v. 11). He wants them to be one in love, loyalty, brotherhood, harmony, peace, and fellowship. They had been in strife that night, contending for places of honor and quarreling about who was the greatest. So Jesus prays for their harmony, their real unity. He wants them to be free from bickering, jealousy, envy, strife, contention, disunity.

His third petition for them is "that they may have

my joy fulfilled in themselves" (v. 13). That night he had said to them, "These things I have spoken to you, that my joy may be in you, and that your joy may be full" (John 15:11). Jesus fills the soul of the true disciple with abiding joy.

He goes on: "I do not pray that thou shouldst take them out of the world, but that thou shouldst keep them from the evil one" (v. 15). They had work to do in the world. They were to live in the world, but not to be corrupted by it. They were to change the world, and not let the world change them. They were not to "be conformed to this world," as Paul suggested later, but to be "transformed by the renewal" of their mind (Rom. 12:2). They were to be like a boat in the water, and not like water in the boat. He prayed that they might be guarded from Satan, the evil one. They were to live Christian lives in spite of their evil environment, in spite of their enemies. They would not escape trouble and persecution, but they would have the loving presence and help of their heavenly Father.

His final petition for those disciples was, "Sanctify them in the truth" (John 17:17). Set them apart, dedicate them, consecrate them, and equip them for their work. "Thy word is truth" (v. 17). That is God's message as revealed in the Holy Scriptures. All truth comes from God in Christ. "God is light and in him is no darkness at all" (1 John 1:5). Jesus said, "I am . . . the truth" (John 14:6). His truth brings freedom from spiritual ignorance and bondage. Jesus then said, "And for their sake I consecrate myself, that they also may be consecrated in truth" (John 17:19). They were to be like Jesus in complete dedication and total involvement. He was sending them into a hostile world, even as his Father had sent him. They needed something of his own dedication if they were to live effective lives.

This prayer for the disciples back there in the first century was answered. He prayed for their safe-keeping, their harmony, their joy, their protection from Satan, and for their dedication. They had their troubles and tribulations, but God was present with them to empower them and use these mightily for his glory. They had differences of opinion, but they worked as brothers in a fellowship of loving service. They had a joy and a love that amazed the world and a dedication that did not waver, even in the face of death.

In this prayer, Jesus prays for all believers of every age (vv. 20–26). He continues his prayer, "I do not pray for these only, but also for those who believe in me through their word" (v. 20). That includes all Christians who have believed because the apostles of the Lord witnessed at home and everywhere they went. That petition includes you and me today.

What is Christ's prayer for us? "That they may all be one; even as thou, Father, art in me, and I in thee, that they also may be in us" (v. 21). This is not a prayer for mechanical union, for union in organization, or for doing away with denominations. All denominations that I am acquainted with are doing some good. In different ways they are ministering to different groups of people and to different classes. This prayer is asking for vital, essential unity in spirit and fellowship. It is a prayer for harmony, peace, cooperation, and brotherhood among all Christians everywhere. It is a petition that we may always be free from narrow contentions, wranglings, prejudices, strife, and unbrotherliness.

Jesus explains the true purpose of this unity: "So that the world may believe that thou hast sent me" (v. 21). The world will never be impressed with Christ until his followers live together in brotherly love, in Christian harmony and peace. Jesus then states another purpose: "So that the world may know that thou hast sent me and hast loved them even as thou hast loved me" (v.23). Our Christian fellowship is proof to the world that God is a God of love and that the love of God unites us in Christ.

Then Jesus prays, saying, "Father, I desire that they also, whom thou hast given me, may be with me where I am, to behold my glory which thou hast given me in thy love for me before the foundation of the world" (v. 24). This is a prayer that all believers may be with Jesus in heaven forever, with him in Paradise, and that we may behold his matchless glory. The most beautiful thing in heaven will be the radiant, majestic grace, beauty, and glory of our Lord and Savior Jesus Christ.

Finally, he prays that "the love with which thou hast loved me may be in them, and I in them" (v. 26). If Christ dwells in us, then love dwells there; if love dwells there, then God dwells there, and we have the very essence of the Christian religion. If we have love, we have everything; but if we have everything else except love, we have nothing.

So this is the Lord's prayer for himself, for his apostles, and for us. It reveals much about him and his glory and shows us how he wants us to live as his followers in today's world.

18

In Gethsemane

"Father, if thou art willing, remove this cup from me; nevertheless not my will, but thine, be done" (Luke 22:42).

Jesus taught his disciples in the model prayer to pray, "Thy will be done, On earth as it is in heaven" (Matt. 6:10). And he observed his own teaching in his life. One of the great and significant events in the life of our Lord was his experience in the garden of Gethsemane, where he prayed on the night before his crucifixion, "My Father, if it be possible, let this cup pass from me; nevertheless, not as I will, but as thou wilt" (Matt. 26:39). He had taken with him into the garden the three disciples who were of the inner circle and had said to them, "My soul is very sorrowful, even to death; remain here, and watch with me" (v. 38). They soon fell asleep as he prayed; so he aroused them and said to Peter, "So, could you not watch with me one hour? Watch and pray that you may not enter into temptation; the spirit indeed is willing, but the flesh is weak" (vv. 40, 41). Then he went aside and prayed again, "My Father, if this cannot pass unless I drink it, thy will be done" (v. 42). He prayed this same prayer a third time. Mark gives a similar account—perhaps the first account ever given—where he tells us that Jesus "began to be greatly distressed and troubled. And he said to them, 'My soul is very sorrowful, even to death; remain here, and watch.' And going a little farther, he fell on the ground and prayed that, if it were possible, the hour might pass from him. And he said, 'Abba, Father, all things are possible to thee; remove this cup from me; yet not what I will, but what thou wilt'" (Mark 14:33–36). The rest of Mark's account is almost exactly like that of Matthew. Luke adds a few more details, saying that Jesus "knelt down" and prayed, "Father, if thou art willing, remove this cup from me; nevertheless not my will, but thine, be done" (Luke 22:42). Luke says that an angel appeared from heaven and strengthened him, and then adds, "And being in an agony he prayed more earnestly; and his sweat became like great drops of blood falling down upon the ground" (v. 44). John does not give us a similar account, although he had said that Jesus prayed shortly before this event, "Now is my soul troubled. And what shall I say? 'Father, save me from this hour'? No, for this purpose I have come to this hour. Father, glorify thy name" (John 12:27). God answered, saying, "I have glorified it, and I will glorify it again" (v. 28).

The New Testament plainly teaches that Jesus always lived by God's will and practiced what he had said, "Pray then like this. . . . Thy will be done, On earth as it is in heaven" (Matt. 6:9, 10).

Jesus said that he came to earth to do the Father's will: "For I have come down from heaven, not to do my own will, but the will of him who sent me" (John 6:38). The writer of Hebrews applied these Old Testament words to Jesus, "'Lo, I have come to do thy will, O God,' as it is written of me in the roll of the book" (Heb. 10:7). Doing God's will meant accomplishing God's work. Jesus said to his disciples, "My food is to do the will of him who sent me, and to accomplish his work" (John 4:34). Doing God's will satisfied Jesus more than food for his body. He had said to his disciples, "I have food to eat of which you do not know" (v. 32). He had just won a sinful woman to discipleship and had given her the living water that would refresh her forevermore. Jesus came to this planet to carry out in every detail the plan and wish and will of his Father in heaven. That will included teaching, preaching, healing, helping, and providing salvation by his atoning death on Calvary and his resurrection from the dead. Just before healing a blind man Jesus had said to the Twelve, "We must work the works of him who sent me, while it is day; night comes, when no one can work" (John 9:4). Later he prayed, "I glorified thee on earth, having accomplished the work which thou gavest me to do" (John 17:4). Doing God's will meant pleasing God in everything. Previously he had said to his enemies and critics, "When you have lifted up the Son of man, then you will know that I am he, and that I do nothing on my own authority but speak thus as the Father taught me. And he who sent me is with me; he has not left me alone, for I always do what is pleasing to him" (John 8:28, 29). Jesus learned God's will as he prayed, for the Father taught him and was always present to guide him in the performance of the divine will. That he pleased God and did his will in everything is shown by God's words at his baptism and at his transfiguration.

On the first occasion God spoke from heaven, "This is my beloved Son, with whom I am well pleased" (Matt. 3:17). On the next occasion he spoke exactly the same words and added, "Listen to him" (Matt. 17:5).

God's will and the will of Jesus were the same. There was perfect unity and harmony. Jesus said, "I can do nothing on my own authority; as I hear, I judge; and my judgment is just, because I seek not my own will but the will of him who sent me" (John 5:30). He sought God's will, even as we must seek it, by prayer and a reverent study of the Holy Bible. In his prayers in Gethsemane he was not seeking to change God's will but to conform to it. That is the wonderful secret of great praying: conformity to the divine will in everything.

Jesus' desire to conform to God's will made him completely unselfish and obedient. He never followed the easy way of personal comfort or freedom from pain and cruel suffering. The devil tempted him to do so, but he was victorious over Satan. Of course Jesus dreaded suffering, and yet he saw joy set before him and glorious victory in the magnetism of his coming cross. His complete dedication to God led him to lay aside his own personal desires and bring them into accord with the desires of his Father. In doing God's will, Jesus could say, "I and the Father are one" (John 10:30). There is no conflict; Jesus wanted what God wanted and was ready to give his all to carry out the will of God who had sent him to earth to do this very thing.

Jesus plainly tells us some things that are God's will. Some of these he learned as he prayed. It is not God's will that anyone should perish. Jesus said that "these little ones"—the children—have angels in heaven. "So it is not the will of my Father who is in heaven that one of these little ones should perish" (Matt. 18:14). We can be confident that it is God's will that all his children should be saved. We can be sure that every little child who dies goes to heaven. Jesus said that we are not to hinder the little children from coming to him "for to such belongs the kingdom of heaven" (Matt. 19:14). It is not God's wish or will that suffering or death should come to any little child. He permits it, but he does not will it.

It is not God's will that Jesus should lose any of those God has given to him. Our Lord said this quite precisely. "For I have come down from heaven, not to do my own will, but the will of him who sent me; and this is the will of him who sent me, that I should lose nothing of all that he has given me, but raise it up at the last day" (John 6:38, 39). He prayed that God would keep in his name all that the Father had given to the Son, even as the Son had kept and guarded them. Only one—Judas Iscariot—perished, and that was because he insisted on having his own selfish will accomplished rather than the will of God. No one can snatch the true Christian from the hand of the Savior or from the hand of the Father.

It is God's expressed will that every believer should have eternal life and be raised from the dead. Our Lord said, "For this is the will of my Father, that every one who sees the Son and believes in him should have eternal life; and I will raise him up at the last day" (v. 40). We must behold Jesus, the Son of God, upon his cross and risen from the dead and upon his throne. We must believe on him personally and sincerely, trusting him, surrendering to him, committing ourselves to him and obeying him. It is always God's will that those who do this be saved. Peter understood this when he said, "The Lord is not slow about his promise as some count slowness, but is forbearing toward you, not wishing that any should perish, but that all should reach repentance" (2 Peter 3:9). Jesus said, "Do not marvel at this; for the hour is coming when all who are in the tombs will hear his voice and come forth, those who have done good, to the resurrection of life, and those who have done evil, to the resurrection of judgment," (John 5:28, 29).

It is God's will that his kingdom come on earth and that his will be done here and now just as it is done in heaven. God plans to make all things new, including heaven and earth (Rev. 21:1).

Jesus saw glorious results from doing God's will. Man enters God's kingdom by doing his will. Jesus declared, "Not every one who says to me, 'Lord, Lord,' shall enter the kingdom of heaven, but he who does the will of my Father who is in heaven" (Matt 7:21). We become spiritually akin to Jesus by doing God's will. Our Savior said, "Here are my mother and my brothers! For whoever does the will of my Father in heaven is my brother, and sister, and mother" (Matt. 12:49, 50). We join God's family by doing the will of the heavenly Father. Our obedience is the sign of our belonging.

Doing God's will enables us to understand the teachings of Jesus, who said, "My teaching is not mine, but his who sent me; if any man's will is to do his will, he shall know whether the teaching is from God or whether I am speaking on my own authority" (John 7:16, 17). If we are really seeking to do God's will, we will be able to recognize the source of divine truth. We recognize Jesus as "a teacher come from God" (John 3:2) and one who has the words of eternal life. Jesus reveals God to us and enables us to know him. Our Lord said, "All things have been delivered to me by my Father; and no one knows the Son except the Father, and no one knows the Father except the Son and any one to whom the Son chooses to reveal him" (Matt. 11:27). The Son chooses to reveal God to all who come to him in faith and take his yoke and learn of him.

The early Christians learned what the will of God was as they listened to Jesus and sought to follow him. James, the Lord's brother, wrote, "Come now, you who say, 'Today or tomorrow we will go into such and such a town and spend a year there and trade and get gain'; whereas you do not know about tomorrow. . . . Instead you ought to say, 'If the Lord wills, we shall live and we shall do this or that'" (James 4:13–15). Paul always sought to know and follow the Lord's will. He wrote to the Corinthians, saying, "But I will come to you soon, if the Lord wills" (1 Cor. 4:19). To the Thessalonians he wrote, "For this is the will of God, your sanctification" (1 Thess. 4:3).

The writer of First John said: "And the world passes away, and the lust of it; but he who does the will of God abides for ever" (1 John 2:17). He also said: "I write this to you who believe in the name of the Son of God, that you may know that you have eternal life. And this is the confidence which we have in him, that if we ask anything according to his will he hears us. And if we know that he hears us in whatever we ask, we know that we have obtained the requests made of him" (1 John 5:13–15).

Jesus prayed in Gethsemane, "Not my will, but thine, be done" and this was his lifelong prayer. It should be the constant prayer of every Christian, for Tennyson was right when he wrote: "Our wills are ours to make them thine."

19

Prayers from the Cross

"Father, forgive them; for they know not what they do" (Luke 23:34).

"My God, my God, why hast thou forsaken me?" (Matt. 27:46).

"Father, into thy hands I commit my spirit" (Luke 23:46).

The supreme hour for which Jesus had come into the world had now fully arrived. It was the hour that God had appointed to manifest his great love for a lost world of sinners. But it was also the hour that the enemies of Jesus had been waiting for from the very beginning of his public ministry.

Our purpose is to listen to Jesus as he prays from his cross. He had said much about prayer, as we have already observed. He had prayed much and often under all kinds of circumstances. Now how would he pray under this intense suffering and in this supreme crisis? Would he now practice what he had preached? Would prayer avail at a time like this?

There are three definite prayers from the cross—there may be five, for the words, "I thirst" (John 19:28) may be interpreted as a prayer. Also the words, "It is finished" (v. 30), were addressed to God. But here we shall examine reverently and carefully his three definite prayers from his cross.

The first is "Father, forgive them; for they know not what they do" (Luke 23:34). Notice that he can still call God "Father" in spite of all that has happened. He had prayed to escape the cross if possible, if salvation could be provided in any other way; but he had determined to do the Father's will and even looked forward to the cross with "joy" (Heb. 12:2), because he knew that it would draw all men to him. It is easy to believe in the fatherhood of God when all goes well, when skies are blue and the sun shines and the flowers bloom. It is easy when we sit in a beautiful church building with Christian friends and hear the gospel preached. When friends are kind, considerate, and loving we feel the very presence of the loving heavenly Father. But how would it be if, like Jesus, we were nailed to a cruel and painful cross? Jesus had been betrayed by one of his own chosen disciples, had been denied by the leader of his apostolic band, and forsaken by most of his followers. He had been abused, mocked, reviled, and condemned by his own countrymen, even the religious leaders. Many others had mocked him, including the soldiers. He had been ridiculed and mocked as a "king." He had been scourged under the order of the governor. The soldiers had plaited a crown of cruel thorns and pressed it upon his brow and had put a reed in his hand as a scepter and dressed him in a military jacket or kingly robe. He had been forced to carry his own cross until he fell exhausted under its heavy weight. The soldiers had nailed his hands and his feet to the cross and had lifted it up and dropped it into the hole prepared for it. He was crucified between two condemned robbers. The soldiers were gambling at the foot of the cross for his seamless robe. If any person was ever justified in hating or being angry and resentful surely Jesus was. He was human, as well as divine, and he suffered as a human being all the agonies of the crucifixion. But in spite of this he could still call God his Father.

Jesus had preached about forgiveness. He had forgiven others. He had said to the paralytic, "My son, your sins are forgiven" (Mark 2:5), and to a very sinful woman, "Your sins are forgiven" (Luke 7:48). He had told Peter to forgive a repenting brother "seventy times seven" times (Matt. 18:22). But are not some offenses unforgivable? It may be easy to forgive when the offense has been slight or when we have not been affected vitally and personally. Jesus, the perfect man, the one who had never committed one act of sin or had one evil thought, one who had always been loving, kind, and helpful, was being cruelly and shamefully and unjustly crucified. The people were too stupid to realize what they were doing. "They know not what they do," said Jesus. But they should have known—that was no excuse for their wicked deed. They were sinning against love, and there was bitter hatred in their hearts.

What was involved in this prayer for forgiveness? Was Jesus asking that God simply wink at this horrible sin? No, of course not! A just and holy God can never wink at sin or treat it lightly. If he could, he never would have permitted this crucifixion. In the eyes of a sinner, sin is not so bad; but in the eyes of a true saint of God, sin is tragically serious. Jesus was praying that

God might lead these people to repentance so that they might find forgiveness when they repented. Some of them later did that very thing and were gloriously saved. Jesus had a right to pray this prayer, for he was dying for their sins, carrying the sin of the world on his own heart. Peter later wrote of Jesus, "He committed no sin; no guile was found on his lips. When he was reviled, he did not revile in return; when he suffered, he did not threaten; but he trusted to him who judges justly. He himself bore our sins in his body on the tree, that we might die to sin and live to righteousness. By his wounds you have been healed" (1 Peter 2:22–24).

What does this wonderful prayer reveal about Jesus? It reveals his gracious spirit of generosity: "They know not what they do." It reveals his great love for sinners. He loved even his enemies, those who were crucifying him. There was no resentment, no hatred, no desire to get even, or to repay these sinners in their own coin. Here we see his willingness to forgive all sinners everywhere if they repent. On the cross he offered pardon to one of the robbers who repented and prayed to be remembered. Jesus is still praying this prayer today for sinners. Forgiveness is written all over his cross. This is the hope for everyone who turns in faith to Jesus Christ.

The second prayer from the cross is "My God, my God, why hast thou forsaken me?" (Matt. 27:46). Matthew says that it was about the ninth hour, that is, three o'clock in the afternoon. It was after three hours of darkness and after six hours of great agony on the cross that Jesus uttered this prayer to God. This is a hard saying to interpret. Did God actually forsake Jesus, his Son? It is a quotation from Psalm 22:1, and Jesus quotes it verbatim. This suggests he had all of it in his mind. This psalm pictures God as holy and a mighty deliverer: "Yet thou art holy, enthroned on the praises of Israel. In thee our fathers trusted; they trusted, and thou didst deliver them. To thee they cried, and were saved; in thee they trusted, and were not disappointed" (vv. 3–5). It is a meaningful psalm of faith and hope and confident assurance.

Now sin always seeks to bring separation. It separates friends. It separates families. It separates sinners from God. Adam and Eve were driven from the Garden of Eden away from the presence of God because of their sin. Isaiah wrote centuries before Christ came: "Behold, the Lord's hand is not shortened, that it cannot save, or his ear dull, that it cannot hear; but your iniquities have made a separation between you and your God, and your sins have hid his face from you so that he does not hear" (Isa. 59:1, 2). A holy, righteous, sinless God cannot look with favor on sin. Sin is contrary to God's very nature. There can be no fellowship between light and darkness. Now Jesus had no sin of his own, but was here bearing the sin of the world. Paul wrote, "For our sake he made him to be sin who knew no sin, so that in him we might become the righteousness of God" (2 Cor. 5:21). In one sense Jesus was so identified with sinners that he was no longer God's Son; and yet God was never closer to his Son than at this moment. The theologians speak of his "substitutionary death," and in a real sense he was our divine Substitute. He died in our place, on our behalf, for our benefit, for our salvation. Here he bore the penalty for sin—separation from God. He cried out in the darkness, and there was no answer, only the hollow echo of his own pitiful cry. That is part of what hell means—separation from God.

How terrible this separation must have been in the

heart and mind of Jesus! He had always enjoyed a glorious and close fellowship with God. God's presence was the most blessed and real thing in his life. But now the sin of the whole world had come between the sinless Son of God and his righteous and holy Father. He looked up for God's face, but there was only darkness, the darkness of midnight, and thunder and lightning and earthquake. How terrible—to cry out in the darkness and hear no answer at all! But that is the penalty for unforgiven sin. Jesus himself said, "On that day many will say to me, 'Lord, Lord, did we not prophesy in your name, and cast out demons in your name, and do many mighty works in your name?' And then will I declare to them, 'I never knew you; depart from me, you evildoers'" (Matt. 7:22, 23).

But there is comfort in this cry: Jesus was separated from God for a few hours so that we might never be separated from him. He endured the darkness and the silence of God that we might never have to endure them. If Jesus Christ is our Savior, we can confidently say with the apostle Paul:

> Who shall separate us from the love of Christ? Shall tribulation, or distress, or persecution, or famine, or nakedness, or peril, or sword? No, in all these we are more than conquerors through him who loved us. For I am sure that neither death, nor life, nor angels, nor principalities, nor things present, nor things to come, nor powers, nor height, nor depth, nor anything else in all creation, will be able to separate us from the love of God in Christ Jesus our Lord. (Rom. 8:35, 37–39)

The last prayer from the cross is "Father, into thy hands I commit my spirit!" (Luke 23:46). "Crying with a loud voice" Jesus said this. "And having said this he breathed his last." This prayer came after his cry of desolation, and so it is a cry of victory! The cloud of sin and darkness passed on, and Jesus saw again his Father's face, and cried with a shout of joy, "Father!" He had trusted his Father all through life. He had never doubted his word or his promises. He had committed himself completely to God. He had an unshakable faith in his heavenly Father, whose will he always did. Now he could say, and did say, "It is finished" (John 19:30). He had done everything in accordance with his Father's will and had provided salvation and redemption and eternal life for everyone who would believe. Now he was ready to come back to the Father's house. Now as he began to taste death for every man (Heb. 2:9) he thought of another verse of Scripture: Psalm 31:5, "Into thy hand I commit my spirit; thou hast redeemed me, O Lord, faithful God." He knew that his Father was beyond the tomb. His God would lead him through the grave to a glad and glorious resurrection morning.

We can have the same assurance if God is our Father and Jesus is our Savior. In life and at death we can commit all to him, knowing that he will keep what we entrust to him until that day when we stand before him in our eternal home. Then he will give us the crown of victory.

If we have truly heard Jesus praying from his cross we can never be the same again. Listen once more with a quiet and reverent mind as Jesus prays: "Father, forgive them; for they know not what they do" (Luke 23:34); "My God, my God, why hast thou forsaken me?" (Matt. 27:46); "Father, into thy hands I commit my spirit" (Luke 23:46).

20

Our Great High Priest

"Since then we have a great high priest who has passed through the heavens, Jesus, the Son of God, let us hold fast our confession" (Heb. 4:14).

We have in previous chapters observed something of what Jesus said about prayer and have seen what the Gospels have said about his praying. We have watched him as he prayed. Now in this last chapter we are to take a look at Jesus our great High Priest.

The word "priest" means a bridge-builder. He is the one who builds a bridge between God and man. He gives man access to God. Jesus had said in John 14:6, "I am the way . . .; no one comes to the Father, but by me." He had also said, "No one knows the Father except the Son and any one to whom the Son chooses to reveal him" (Matt. 11:27). Someone has pointed out a general characteristic of the priest and of the prophet. "The priest speaks to God on behalf of man, while the prophet speaks to man the message of God." Well,

Jesus was both priest and prophet. He speaks to God for man. He opens the way to God by sacrifice.

The priest was at the center of the Jewish religion. There were many priests but only one high priest at any given time. All the Jewish priests were from the line of Aaron and the tribe of Levi. On the Day of Atonement the high priest entered the Holy of Holies behind the veil in the temple to intercede for himself and for his people. He made sacrifices for himself and for the people. But the Lord Jesus Christ was crucified, the Gospels tell us, "And behold, the curtain of the temple was torn in two, from top to bottom" (Matt. 27:51; Mark 15:38; Luke 23:45). This signified that now every man has access to God through Christ, our High Priest, who is, as Paul told Timothy, "one mediator between God and men, the man Christ Jesus, who gave himself as a ransom for all, the testimony to which was borne at the proper time" (1 Tim. 2:5, 6). What kind of High Priest is Jesus? He is described in the book of Hebrews.

Jesus is one who "had to be made like his brethren in every respect, so that he might become a merciful and faithful high priest in the service of God, to make expiation for the sins of the people" (Heb. 2:17). The writer continues in the next verse: "For because he himself has suffered and been tempted, he is able to help those who are tempted." We have already studied his temptations and seen how he overcame Satan and sin and how he began his ministry in keeping with God's will.

> Since then we have a great high priest who has passed through the heavens, Jesus, the Son of God, let us hold fast our confession. For we have not a high priest who

> is unable to sympathize with our weaknesses, but one who in every respect has been tempted as we are, yet without sinning. Let us then with confidence draw near to the throne of grace, that we may receive mercy and find grace to help in time of need. (Heb. 4:14–16)

In this meaningful passage we learn that the sufferings and temptations of Jesus are representative of the sufferings and temptations of all men. When we are tempted and when we suffer, we cannot say to him, Lord, you just do not know what I have had to bear and how I was tempted. Jesus can say, and he does say through his Holy Spirit: Yes, I understand fully. I passed through similar sufferings and all the temptations within the power of Satan to bring. I understand fully, but I can also help you if you will "draw near to the throne of grace" and accept the help that I offer you. Jesus was merciful to those who came to him seeking help. He is the one who said, "Blessed are the merciful, for they shall obtain mercy" (Matt. 5:7). He showed mercy to the robber who was crucified by his side and promised this repenting man a home in heaven with the Lord. He said to Paul, who prayed to him repeatedly about a thorn in the flesh, "My grace is sufficient for you, for my power is made perfect in weakness" (2 Cor. 12:9). Jesus was faithful to God and fulfilled his divine plan in making expiation for the sins of the people as he gave himself upon the cross. Our great High Priest offers us understanding, sympathy, mercy, and help whenever we come to his throne of grace.

The author of Hebrews goes on to say, "Therefore, holy brethren, who share in a heavenly call, consider Jesus, the apostle and high priest of our confession. He was faithful to him who appointed him" (Heb. 3:1, 2).

He was God's missionary and apostle to this planet. Jesus repeatedly said in John's Gospel, and elsewhere, that God had sent him into the world. God had sent him as a representative and as a priest or bridge-builder between God and man. And Jesus came to earth and was perfectly obedient to his Father, making God's will the one great law of his life. Moses was faithful as a servant in God's house, "But Christ was faithful over God's house as a son" (v. 6), and we who are Christians are the household of the faith, or the family of God.

Our High Priest "has passed through the heavens, Jesus, the Son of God" (Heb. 4:14). He has been exalted to the highest heaven and has been given the highest honor in heaven. It was God the Father who exalted him. "Christ did not exalt himself to be made a high priest, but was appointed by him who said to him, 'Thou art my Son, today I have begotten thee'" (5:5). In 5:7–9 there seems to be an echo of Gethsemane and of other sufferings of Jesus: "In the days of his flesh, Jesus offered up prayers and supplications, with loud cries and tears, to him who was able to save him from death, and he was heard for his godly fear. Although he was a Son, he learned obedience through what he suffered; and being made perfect he became the source of eternal salvation to all who obey him." Jesus was human as well as divine, and yet he was the only perfect human being who could become the source of salvation to all other human beings.

We are reminded several times in Hebrews that Jesus was a "high priest after the order of Melchizedek" (Heb. 5:6, 10; 6:20). This strange character is described as "king of Salem, priest of the Most High God" who blessed Abraham, to whom the latter gave tithes. He is called "king of righteousness, and then he is also king of Salem, that is, king of peace. He is without father or mother or genealogy, and has neither beginning of days nor end of life, but resembling the Son of God he continues a priest for ever" (Heb. 7:1–3). Abraham was the father of the Levites, from whom the priests had come. They alone were to be the recipients of tithes. But here, still in the loins of Abraham, they gave tithes to one who was not of the tribe of Levi.

The old levitical priestly system was imperfect and had to be replaced by a new system. It was necessary for a new priest to arise from a new order, not the order of Aaron from whom the Levites came. Jesus came from the tribe of Judah. His priesthood is forever, whereas in the old order the priests died and had to be replaced. But Jesus, our High Priest, was appointed by God with an oath sworn by himself, for there is none higher. "We have this as a sure and steadfast anchor of the soul, a hope that enters into the inner shrine behind the curtain, where Jesus has gone as a forerunner on our behalf, having become a high priest for ever after the order of Melchizedek" (Heb. 6:19, 20). The old covenant of law could not save. The people broke the covenant every time they broke the law. There had to be a new covenant, based upon love and grace, one that could never fail. Jesus became "a priest, not according to a legal requirement concerning bodily descent but by the power of an indestructible life" (Heb. 7:16). "This makes Jesus the surety of a better covenant" (v. 22).

Jesus "holds his priesthood permanently, because he continues for ever. Consequently he is able for all time to save those who draw near to God through him, since he always lives to make intercession for them" (vv. 24, 25). The Lord prayed for his disciples while he was with them in the flesh. Now he prays for all who come to God through him. As he prayed for Simon

Peter, he prays for us today. What a blessed assurance: he lives forever to intercede for all who come to God through him, our great High Priest.

Jesus is described as "a high priest, holy, blameless, unstained, separated from sinners, exalted above the heavens" (v. 26). We are told there were 142 physical blemishes that could bar the levitical priests, but there was not one blemish in our perfect High Priest, Jesus Christ, our Lord.

He did not need, like other priests, to offer sacrifices for his own sins as well as for the sins of the people. He made one complete and all-sufficient atonement for the sin in every age. "He did this once for all when he offered up himself" (v. 27). He was perfect forever and needed no sacrifice for himself, since he had no sin.

Our High Priest is the minister of the sanctuary and the true tabernacle. The author of this wonderful epistle says: "Now the point in what we are saying is this: we have such a high priest, one who is seated at the right hand of the throne of the Majesty in heaven, a minister in the sanctuary and the true tent which is set up not by man but by the Lord" (Heb. 8:1, 2). Christ "obtained a ministry which is as much more excellent than the old as the covenant he mediates is better, since it is enacted on better promises" (v. 6). The first covenant was based on law, which man could not keep. The new covenant is in the heart and mind of God's people. In this covenant they find mercy and pardon for their sin.

Christ Jesus, our High Priest, has obtained eternal redemption for us. "But when Christ appeared as a high priest . . . he entered once for all into the Holy Place, taking not the blood of goats and calves but his own blood, thus securing an eternal redemption. For if the sprinkling of defiled persons with the blood of goats and bulls and with the ashes of a heifer sanctifies for the purification of the flesh, how much more shall the blood of Christ, who through the eternal Spirit offered himself without blemish to God, purify your conscience from dead works to serve the living God" (Heb. 9:11–14). This is the new covenant in his blood which Jesus speaks of at the Last Supper (Matt. 26:28).

Our High Priest, Christ Jesus, has gone back to heaven, from whence he came, "Now to appear in the presence of God on our behalf. . . . he has appeared once for all at the end of the age to put away sin by the sacrifice of himself. . . . Christ, having been offered once to bear the sins of many, will appear a second time, not to deal with sin but to save those who are eagerly waiting for him" (Heb. 9:24, 26, 28). Since the blood of animals could never really take away any man's sins, Jesus came and offered his own body on the cross. "But when Christ had offered for all time a single sacrifice for sins, he sat down at the right hand of God. For by a single offering he has perfected for all time those who are sanctified" (Heb. 10:12, 14).

What does it mean for us today to have such a High Priest as Jesus? In Hebrews we read of several important benefits we can enjoy.

"Let us then with confidence draw near to the throne of grace, that we may receive mercy and find grace to help in time of need" (Heb. 4:16). We can with perfect assurance pray to our wonderful Savior and receive the help he graciously offers. We should always obey him, "the source of eternal salvation" (Heb. 5:9). We cannot expect him to answer our prayers unless we are willing to obey him.

Again, our author tells us, "Since we have a great high priest over the house of God, let us draw near with a true heart in full assurance of faith, with our hearts sprinkled clean from an evil conscience and our bodies washed with pure water. Let us hold fast the confession of our hope without wavering, for he who promised is faithful; and let us consider how to stir up one another to love and good works, not neglecting to meet together, as is the habit of some, but encouraging one another, and all the more as you see the Day drawing near" (Heb. 10:21–25).

We are to keep our eyes fixed on Jesus and do his will. "Let us run with perseverance the race that is set before us, looking to Jesus the pioneer and perfecter of our faith, who for the joy that was set before him endured the cross, despising the shame, and is seated at the right hand of the throne of God" (Heb. 12:1, 2).

Since we have come "to Jesus, the mediator of a new covenant (v. 24) . . . "Therefore let us be grateful for receiving a kingdom that cannot be shaken, and thus let us offer to God acceptable worship, with reverence and awe" (v. 28). "Through him then let us continually offer up a sacrifice of praise to God, that is, the fruit of lips that acknowledge his name. Do not neglect to do good and to share what you have, for such sacrifices are pleasing to God" (Heb. 13:15, 16). How about that for a religion that is indeed relevant today!

The beautiful benediction found in Hebrews 13:20, 21 makes a fitting close for this book. "Now may the God of peace who brought again from the dead our Lord Jesus, the great shepherd of the sheep, by the blood of the eternal covenant, equip you with everything good that you may do his will, working in you that which is pleasing in his sight, through Jesus Christ; to whom be glory for ever and ever. Amen."